Leading Picasso

The Art and Science of Managing IT, Part 3

A Reference Guide for IT Leaders

Stephen K. Wiggins CIO

Kenneth C. Abernethy PhD

Suzanne B. Summers PhD

ISBN: 1500188611
ISBN 13: 9781500188610
Library of Congress Control Number: 2014911465
CreateSpace Independent Publishing Platform
North Charleston, South Carolina

Leading Picasso

*The Art and Science of Managing IT,
Part 3*

Contents

Acknowledgments   xi

Preface   xiii

Part I: A Framework for IT Leadership

1   Introduction: The Art and Science of Leading IT   3
     Two Types of Leaders   *5*
     A Leader's Distinctive and Complementary Systems of Action   *8*
     A Leader's Impact on Organizational Culture   *12*
     General Qualities of a Leader   *14*

2   Picasso on a Schedule and Managing Picasso: Concepts Review   17
     The IT-OSD Model   *17*
     The Hierarchical Matrix   *21*
     Running IT as a Business   *30*

3   Fundamentals of Leadership Development   37
     Personal Attributes for Effective Leadership   *38*
     Leadership Development for Organizational Success   *43*
     Leadership Competencies for the Matrix and the Hierarchy   *50*
     Why Leadership Matters   *58*

Part II: Culture and Leadership

4   Build and Nurture Culture   67
     What is Culture?   *68*
     Building Culture   *70*

   The Importance of Culture   *72*

   Three Pillars of an IT Culture   *74*

5   The Face of Culture   83

   The Levels of Culture   *83*

   Culture Expressed in Symbols   *85*

   Culture Expressed in Environment   *87*

   Culture Expressed in Observable Behavior   *93*

   Culture Expressed in Guiding Principles   *96*

   Culture Expressed in Underlying Assumptions   *104*

Part III: Vision and Leadership

6   Create a Compelling Vision   109

   What is Vision?   *109*

   Elements of a Compelling Vision   *110*

   Vision and Strategy Revisited   *116*

Part IV: Transformative Change and Leadership

7   Change, Vision, and Culture   125

   The Nature of Transformative Change   *126*

   Compelling Vision Inspires Change   *128*

   The Right Culture Enables Change   *131*

   Developing a Learning Culture: An Example   *136*

8   The Leader's Purpose   149

   Preparing for Change   *150*

   Leveraging Culture and Vision   *154*

   Leading Change   *156*

Part V: Applying the Art and Science of Leadership

9   The Hierarchy and Matrix Leadership Cycles   163

   The Hierarchy Leadership Cycle   *164*

The Matrix Leadership Cycle   *166*
Learning through Leadership Simulations   *169*

10 A Case Study in Transformative Change   173
    Change Drivers   *173*
    The Vision for Change   *176*
    From Vision to Strategy   *181*
    An Additional Change Driver   *195*
    Leverage the Culture   *203*
    The Rainbow Chart of Processes: Definitions   *204*

References   233

Appendix: Behaviors Characterizing the Differentiating Competencies for IT   235

Acknowledgments

In writing the *Picasso* book series, we have benefited from the help and support of numerous people, and the ideas captured here are distilled from a great many experiences and thoughtful conversations. Colleagues who have shared those experiences and engaged in those conversations will no doubt see their influences within these pages.

But there have been so many of these experiences and conversations that we would surely leave out important contributors if we tried to recount them all by name. And so, with apologies for not mentioning all of you, and with the assurance that the absence of names doesn't mean we are any less in your debt, we sincerely thank the following groups.

The intelligence, dedication, and hard work of the management team and professional staff of the Information Systems Division at BlueCross BlueShield of South Carolina have produced the incredible success story on which much of the material in these pages is based, and we offer sincere thanks to all for your remarkable efforts. The participation of the management team and selected members of the professional staff in two important programs over a number of years has provided the foundation for the extended exploration of the ideas presented in this series.

To all the participants of the Summer Institutes presented by the Institute for the Management of IT at Furman University and the Executive Leadership Summit program organized and guided by Jack Zenger, CEO of Zenger Folkman, and his staff, we thank you for your openness to learning, your enthusiastic engagement in meaningful discussions, your effective application of the concepts presented, and your thoughtful feedback on how the experiences could be improved.

Of course, those great learning experiences were also the consequence of the able and dedicated faculty and facilitators who presented concepts and guided the participants' exploration and application of these, and so to this outstanding group goes our sincere thanks for your professionalism, enthusiasm, preparation, insights, as well as your own willingness to learn. Further, the support staff, both at Furman and in the I/S Division, have worked tirelessly to make these experiences as rewarding as possible, and we thank them sincerely for that.

Finally, while the contributions of these groups have been invaluable in helping us formulate, revise, and refine this material, we take sole responsibility for any and all errors and misrepresentations that might have survived the final edit.

Steve Wiggins,
Ken Abernethy
Suzy Summers

Preface

This book is the third in a trilogy on the theme of the art and science of managing an information technology (IT) company. In our first book, *Picasso on a Schedule: The Art and Science of Managing IT, Part 1* (hereafter referred to as simply *Picasso on a Schedule*), we introduced and explored a set of concepts that we believe are fundamental for the management of information technology (IT) as a successful business. These concepts apply both to IT companies that are positioned within the distinct IT industry comprised of IT-related companies, as well as to IT organizations or companies that are positioned within other industries ("businesses within a business").

To set the context, for our purposes *information technology (IT)* is defined to include three major components. First, IT traditionally involves the study, design, development, implementation, support, and management of computer-based information systems. Second, these systems typically enable the converting, storing, protecting, processing, transmitting, and retrieving of data for one of two major purposes: (1) *data processing*, which turns data into useful, meaningful, accessible information; and (2) *process automation*, which controls machinery and/or processes to reduce the need for human sensory and mental intervention in work. And third, IT can be thought of as the formation of a collection of *IT products*, comprising computer hardware and/or software, and *IT services*, comprising telecommunications hardware, software, and services.

In *Picasso on a Schedule* we introduced the organizational structure called the *Hierarchical Matrix*. The purpose of the Hierarchical Matrix is to enable an IT business to operate as a resource-scarce organization (i.e., operate with efficiency), while producing solutions for its clients as if it were resource-rich (i.e., operate with effectiveness). A moment's thought reveals that efficiency and effectiveness can often be in tension, and so the goal for any organization is to find the right *balance* between these two to produce the required value for its clients. The beauty and power of the Hierarchical Matrix structure is that its *self-correcting mechanisms* allow it to achieve such equilibrium naturally in most cases.

Understanding and managing the complex nature of large human organizations is critical to achieving the proper balance between efficiency and effectiveness. To aid in the understanding of this complexity and to enable its proper management, the Hierarchical Matrix structure draws a clear distinction between the responsibilities of the technical workforce (the resources of the Matrix) and management (the resources of the Hierarchy).

In essence, this distinction hinges on the following division of responsibilities. In the Hierarchical Matrix, it is the job of the technical workforce to provide the competence to ensure the effective and timely completion of excellent work, while management is responsible for ensuring the quality of both the workforce itself and the technical infrastructure it utilizes, and the efficient combination of these two in achieving the strategic objectives of the IT organization's clients.

In the second book of the series, *Managing Picasso: The Art and Science of Managing IT, Part 2* (hereafter referred to as simply *Managing Picasso)*, we describe the fundamental concepts and processes that support the management responsibilities within the Hierarchical component of the Hierarchical Matrix organizational structure. The Hierarchy comprises the system of actions referred to as *management,* which focuses on activities that produce a degree of predictability and order for the IT organization.

The mission of the Hierarchy is to provide a framework for the high level of business and technical competence necessary for management to accomplish two primary outcomes. The first outcome is to create and manage a workforce that produces excellent and innovative products and services to its clients. The second, and equally important outcome, is to run IT as a successful business. To accomplish this mission, managers in the Hierarchy must understand the peculiar nature of software itself, possess the technical competence to deal with the creative and open-ended nature of IT work, and be proficient in the common business practices and governance principles under which other non-IT businesses operate.

In the current book, *Leading Picasso: The Art and Science of Managing IT, Part 3* (hereafter referred to as simply *Leading Picasso*), we will focus on the importance of leadership, within both the Hierarchy *and* the Matrix, in successfully implementing the concepts discussed in the first two books. Though leadership is surely based on many intangibles, we believe that being an effective leader in an IT company also depends on an understanding and mastery of a set of well-defined and interconnected principles that enable and energize great IT leadership. These principles comprise the foundation for creating a compelling and authentic *Vision* and for building and sustaining a *Culture* that provides the agility and underlying strength to maintain success in achieving that vision in the face of the rapid, often unpredictable, and potentially disorienting change that characterizes the IT industry.

This book is organized as an accessible reference guide to this connected set of leadership principles that will enable the development of effective leaders in both the Hierarchy and the Matrix. Because the book is intended as reference guide, we have adopted a much more practical focus for the ideas and concepts being explored than we used in *Picasso on a Schedule*. In laying the foundation for this series in *Picasso on a Schedule*, we framed the discussion largely at the conceptual level, referring only occasionally and briefly to the application of the major ideas. In essence, we believe that *Picasso on a Schedule* has provided much of the conceptual context for the other two books in the series. Hence we have strived to make the current presentation less conceptual and more applied.

Toward this end, as we did with *Managing Picasso*, we have chosen a different format for the presentation, employing an extended outline layout that will allow the reader to more easily locate and grasp specific practical topics of interest. Though an IT leader could profitably read the book from start to finish for a complete introduction to the framework of principles being presented, we believe that an additional value of the book is as a reference to these various principles, allowing the IT leader to quickly access more detailed descriptions when desired and some practical tips about how they might be applied.

The ideas explored in this series have emerged from a thirteen-year collaboration between the authors in creating professional development programs to support and enhance the remarkable success of a particular IT company—the Information Systems (I/S) Division of BlueCross BlueShield of South Carolina. This success has been impressive. The I/S Division of BlueCross BlueShield of South Carolina operates as a business within a business in the context of the BlueCross BlueShield of South Carolina family of insurance businesses. Since the early 1990s, the I/S Division has had steady and sustained growth, evolving from an organization of 300 people to one employing more than 2,000 people, and increasing the total number of annual online healthcare transactions completed from just under 700 million to over 20 billion. As of this writing, the I/S Division processes approximately 10% of the total Health Care expenditure in the United States.

However, we want to emphasize that this series is about more than one company's success. Indeed, it is our hope and belief that anyone facing the challenge of managing and leading an IT company, an IT unit, or large IT projects will find ideas and concepts throughout the series that resonate with their experiences and that will provoke them to think in new and more productive ways about the work they do. Furthermore, it is our belief that presenting a concrete example of how these ideas and concepts have been successfully applied in the I/S Division will provide valuable guidance to those readers who wish to adapt them to their own environments.

Finally, as we did with *Picasso on a Schedule* and *Managing Picasso*, we invite the readers' responses to this material as well as any relevant suggestions, inquiries, and questions. And we would be happy to provide more detail about the application of the concepts within the I/S Division of BlueCross BlueShield of South Carolina upon request.

Part I
A Framework for IT Leadership

Chapter 1

Introduction:
The Art and Science of Leading IT

A leader can be defined as a person who shows others the way to accomplish a goal or outcome for the success of an organization. While leaders play an important part in an organization's current success by helping devise successful strategies and ensuring that the resources necessary for their implementation are present. The real work of leadership is to ensure that the organization's success is sustained in the future. To accomplish this, leaders must lead the organization in building the capabilities, and the agility to exploit those capabilities, that enable it to adapt to changing business conditions. Without the necessary capabilities and agility, these changing conditions can render the strategies of today's successful IT organization ineffective, or even counterproductive, in tomorrow's business climate.

In other words, though interested in, and supportive of, the efforts an IT organization is exerting to meet its current business challenges, leaders must always be looking toward the future. They must try to identify the kinds of potential changes that are implicit in the external environment, focusing on those that represent opportunities and threats to today's successes, and preparing the organization to adapt to those changes successfully and with as little disruption as possible.

In *Managing Picasso* [2], we identified two major challenges facing any information technology (IT) organization. One is the identification and use of operational and administrative processes that the IT organization must perform to produce a desired outcome. The second is the identification and use of basic IT roles that must be successfully fulfilled as they relate to these processes. Meeting both these challenges requires excellent leaders. But whether an information technology (IT) organization's mission is the creating, maintaining, executing, or hosting of self-created systems, the selecting, installing, executing, or hosting of vendor-supplied systems, or some combination of the two, at the heart of every computer system is the software that supports the specific requirements of a given user. And so to achieve excellent IT leadership, IT leaders must first truly understand the fundamental nature of software and its development.

With such an understanding, leaders are equipped to better identify how anticipated changes in the business environment could potentially impact the organization, and how the fundamental nature of software and its development will frame and mold the organization's possible responses to these impacts. More specifically, such understanding allows leaders the chance to wisely position the IT organization's resources and processes to be robust across a large spectrum of possible change. While charisma and personality can enhance a leader's effectiveness, these are never a substitute for a deep and fundamentally sound understanding of what an IT enterprise really is, and how this reality defines its inherent possibilities and limitations.

In *Picasso on a Schedule* [1], we discussed at some length how software development is in fact a complex combination of art and science. This dichotomous nature of the craft of software development—part art, part science—has led to many misunderstandings and misconceptions in both the software user/purchaser and IT communities. We believe that recognizing and accepting this inevitable dichotomy are the first steps toward effectively leading an information technology organization.

Software development is distinguished, and greatly complicated, by the fact that software is an *abstraction*. Because a software product is entirely abstract, there is no physical-world frame of reference to provide an intuitive understanding of the product and its associated construction process. This lack of a physical frame of reference necessitates a different management approach to estimating required effort, tracking progress, measuring productivity, and understanding and accommodating the inherent uncertainties of purely creative work. The underlying reality is that because software development embodies both art and science/engineering, so does being an effective leader. To illustrate this dichotomy within IT leaders, we offer the following observations about two basic types of IT leaders, both of which are required for success.

Two Types of Leaders

The IT-OSD (Organizational System Design) Model, illustrated in Figure 1.1, was introduced in *Picasso on a Schedule* and discussed further in *Managing Picasso*. (We'll provide a brief overview/review of the IT-OSD Model's essential components in the next chapter.) In short, it can be used to help IT organizations better evaluate and understand the connections between various high-level organizational design factors, as well as the organization's connections to the external business environment.

The Hierarchical Matrix was also introduced in *Picasso on a Schedule* as a solution for one of the high-level design choices, namely organizational structure. The Hierarchical Matrix structure draws a clear distinction between the responsibilities of the technical workforce (the resources of the Matrix) and management (the resources of the Hierarchy).

In essence, this distinction hinges on the following division of responsibilities. In the Hierarchical Matrix, it is the job of the technical workforce (the Matrix) to provide the competence to ensure the effective and timely completion of excellent work, while management (The Hierarchy) is responsible for ensuring the quality of both the workforce itself and the technical infrastructure it utilizes, and the efficient combination of these two in achieving the strategic objectives of the IT organization's clients.

In other words, the IT-OSD model provides members of the Hierarchy and Matrix a decision-making framework within which they can maintain and support the creativity necessary for excellence, imposing appropriate structure and controls to ensure a balanced focus on technical and business competence, and better anticipate and plan for changes arising in the external environment. For ongoing success, the IT-OSD Model itself must be flexible and adaptive enough to support an evolutionary and systematic approach to adaptive change. Overseeing such adaption and evolution is the job of both the Hierarchy and Matrix leadership teams of the organization.

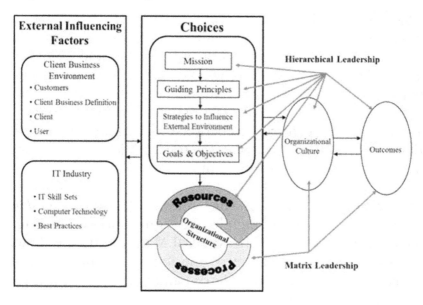

Figure 1.1: *The Information Technology Organizational System Design Model*

As a decision-making framework, the IT-OSD Model provides a basis for the *science* of IT leadership—a systematic way to evaluate the impact of various factors on the achievement of the desired organizational outcomes. However, the actual utilization of the model involves as much art as science. To illustrate this point, we will discuss how *art* is inherent in the application of two essential categories of leadership within the model: *Hierarchical Leadership* and *Matrix Leadership* as illustrated in Figure 1.1.

Consider the bottom section of the organizational choices component of the IT-OSD Model as illustrated in Figure 1.2. The choices depicted focus on blending and leveraging resources and processes through the organizational structure. Certainly, methods for accomplishing this blending can be worked out in theory; that is, the science can be described. But, applying that science means optimizing the work of *people*, the primary resource within software development.

Figure 1.2: *Choices that Comprise the Matrix within the IT-OSD Model*

As we will explore in more detail later, such application requires excellent communication, empathy, persuasion, motivation, flexibility, adaptation, and support—in short a keen understanding of human nature which involves at least as much art as science. As shown in Figure 1.1, Hierarchy Leaders have the responsibility of *efficiently using the organization's resources: human, financial and other* to ensure *that the Matrix produces outcomes that satisfy the goals and objectives derived from the IT organization's strategies.* We'll refer to this type of leadership as *Hierarchical Leadership*, which emanates from traditional command and control authority.

In order for the Matrix to be successful in meeting the challenge described above the leadership of the Hierarchy must be reinforced and augmented by leaders *within the Matrix itself.* As indicated in Figure 1.1, we'll refer to this type of leadership as *Matrix Leadership.* Note that Matrix Leadership emanates from the authority associated with a given IT role and must be applied situation-by-situation by those in the Matrix as they conduct the outcome-driven work of the organization.

A Leader's Distinctive and Complementary Systems of Action

The use of the IT-OSD Model by the Information Systems Division of BlueCross BlueShield of South Carolina has resulted in the creation of *two integrated systems of action—referred to as **Management** and **Leadership** respectively—to be used by both Hierarchical and Matrix Leaders* to produce award-winning application systems, and a world-class information, communication and technology infrastructure in support of a wide variety of clients and their customers.

Systems of Action

It is important to an IT organization's long term success that all employees understand the purpose of an organization's processes and how to effectively work within its boundaries. To successfully utilize the processes an organization needs people in roles who are highly skilled at what they do. Those in certain roles required to support the framework of processes associated with the Hierarchy and Matrix will need to master the two distinctive and complementary systems of action in order to be successful leaders within the Hierarchy or Matrix teams. Hierarchy Leaders will focus these systems of action on different activities than Matrix Leaders. The primary differences are that Matrix Leaders drive work and work results; and Hierarchy Leaders ensure efficient use of the organization's resources—human, financial, and other—as well as prepare the organization for future success.

It is also important to note that for either type of leader to be successful, each must fully understand the Rainbow Chart of Matrix Processes. In addition, to work effectively in an organization, every leader must understand and embrace three fundamental concepts:

- Skills are what an individual offers

- Process is how work is done

- Culture is their organization's behavior

The goal is for all leaders to gain the skills of the two complementary systems of action and apply them within the boundaries and rules of the organization's processes. [3]

Note on terminology

The words *management* and *leadership* are used in two distinct ways in this book:

1) Referencing the specific *complementary systems of action* (just introduced and to be explained below), and

2) Referencing a *generic position or function* within an organization.

To distinguish these two uses, from this point forward in the book when the reader sees the words *Management* or *Leadership* italicized and first letter capitalized, the words will be referring to the one of the complementary systems of action. Otherwise the words will be referring to a generic position or function within an organization.

The Management System of Action

The *Management* system of action comprises:

- A distinctive system of action to *cope with complexity*:
  - Requiring a thorough understanding of organizational structure and processes to effectively produce a degree of predictability and order
  - Utilizing the framework of processes associated with the Hierarchy and the Matrix that keep a complicated system of people and technology running smoothly
- Controlling or directing day-to-day business processes to accomplish a desired result through formal authority emanating from traditional command and control for the Hierarchy or from the authority associated with a given IT role within the Matrix.

The Leadership System of Action

The *Leadership* system of action comprises:

- A distinctive system of action to *cope with change:*
  - Requiring a set of skills and behaviors that constitute the strengths that actually define a leader and drives the *effective employment of culture and vision*
  - Utilizing a set of processes that help direct, align, and inspire actions on the part of large numbers of people to:
    - Organize in the first place
    - Adapt their organization to significantly changing circumstances
- Guiding or inspiring other people to accomplish a desired result through *influence*

Management Activities

The *Management* system of action focuses on three main categories of activities:

- **Provide Information**. Establish and maintain a communication link for constantly receiving and giving information orally or in written form that must be successfully executed by people performing roles as defined within the framework of processes associated with the Hierarchy and the Matrix for the effective functioning of the IT organization.

- **Make Decisions**. Be responsible for the making of the many decisions which become the basis of action to be executed by people performing various roles as defined within the framework of processes associated with the Hierarchy and the Matrix to produce successful outcomes.

    ○ The decision processes must include an *escalation process* which can be used to resolve conflict over work issues that the various roles being performed cannot resolve locally

    ○ *Escalation should always focus on finding the resolution that best serves the goals and objectives of the IT organization*

- **Encourage Inter-Personal Interactions.** Encourage activities to develop and maintain good relations in support of positive interactions among the people performing various roles within the framework of processes associated with the Hierarchy and the Matrix in achieving the organization's goals.

Leadership Activities

Hierarchy Leaders must focus on the following activity associated with the *Leadership* system of action in order to establish direction for the organization:

- **Establish Vision and Strategies**. Hierarchy Leaders must provide:
  - ○ Vision, which:
    - ▪ Refers to a picture of the future with some implicit or explicit commentary
    - ▪ Must be described in five minutes or less, and solicits a reaction that signifies both understanding and interest, on why people should strive to create that future
  - ○ Strategies, which provide the logic by which the vision can be achieved

We stated earlier that both Hierarchy and Matrix Leaders must have a keen understanding of human nature in order to effectively apply the arts of persuasion, motivation, flexibility, adaptation, and support that are necessary to enable those in the Matrix to successfully produce the organization's outcomes. Therefore, both Hierarchical and Matrix Leaders must focus on the following activities associated with the *Leadership* system of action:

- **Align People with the Vision**. Communicate clear direction in words and deeds to all those whose cooperation may be needed to achieve the vision

- **Motivate, Inspire, and Energize People**. Motivate, inspire and energize all those whose cooperation may be needed to achieve the vision, so that they can overcome obstacles that get in the way of the achieving the vision

A Leader's Impact on Organizational Culture

As illustrated in Figure 1.1, Hierarchical Leadership responsibilities are focused on the most fundamental choices an organization must make, specifically *its mission, its guiding principles, its strategies to influence the external environment,* and *its goals and objectives.*

Those fundamental choices that Hierarchy Leaders make have great influence on the *organizational culture* which determines the essential nature of the organization's workplace. Organizational culture in turn has great influence on the outcomes the organization produces.

Further, and most importantly, culture is inextricably tied to the organization's ultimate capabilities and agility. Hence laying the foundation for and nurturing the organizational culture is one of a Hierarchy Leader's most important responsibilities to be accomplished through the execution of the *Leadership* system of action. In addition, the *Leadership* system of action calls for Matrix Leaders to appreciate, and know how to utilize, the organizational culture within which the work is being conducted.

Organizational culture is an intangible entity, a kind of "personality of the organization in action," which:

- Is derived from, and synthesizes, the mission, guiding principles, and strategies that the organization has adopted

- Provides through this synthesis a context within which people align their individual efforts with organizational ambitions through an understanding of how they are expected to behave most of the time

- Enables Matrix Leaders to optimize the utilization of the Matrix process framework for the efficient and effective completion of the work that achieves the desired organizational outcomes

A central two-fold philosophy for the success of the Matrix is:

- **Individual Accountability**, which:
  - Is defined and reinforced by the inter-connected roles which ensures that an IT organization has the expertise to carry out its mission-critical processes

○ Provides all those in the Matrix with clear direction about their own accountabilities within their individual role, as well as the work results they should expect from those in other roles

- **Shared Responsibility**, which:

   ○ Recognizes that because of the creative and unpredictable nature of IT work, a rigid adherence to roles accountability will rarely be sufficient to successfully complete a work effort

   ○ Emphasizes that *teams win and teams lose,* and hence places the collective responsibility for success on the *team*

   ○ Provides the freedom and responsibility for those within the Matrix process framework to get the help they need to successfully complete their work

   ○ Requires Matrix Leaders:

      ▪ To proactively and skillfully navigate and negotiate the various obstacles that stand in the way of success

      ▪ Recognize when removing these obstacles requires help from the Hierarchy, and employ the Escalation Process to get that help

General Qualities of a Leader

Whether we are considering Hierarchy or Matrix Leaders, there are some high-level qualities that we expect any leader to have. The priority of importance of these qualities in a leader will depend on the level of leadership needed as well as the responsibilities that the leader has, but all are important to varying degrees in leaders at all levels. Table 1.1 lists some of the most important of these qualities, gives a succinct definition of each, and offers some hallmark descriptions that would indicate that an individual possesses such qualities.

Table 1.1: General Qualities and Hallmarks of a Leader

Quality	Definition	Hallmarks	
Intelligence	The most complex mental capacity of an organism for cognition, indicating its efficacy in goal-oriented interactions with its environment.	Learning Reasoning Planning Abstraction	Comprehension Problem solving Idea formation Language
Toughness	Ability to withstand great strain without tearing or breaking	Strong Resilient	
Determination	Firmness of purpose, resolve	Decisive	
Vision	The faculty of insight	Imaginable Desirable Feasible	Focused Flexible Communicable
Self-Awareness	The ability to recognize and understand your moods, emotions, and drives, as well as their effect on others	Self-confidence Realistic self-assessment Self-deprecating sense of humor	
Self-Regulation	The ability to control or redirect disruptive impulses and moods	Trustworthiness and integrity Comfort with ambiguity Openness to change	
Motivation	A passion to work for reasons that go beyond money or status	Strong drive to achieve Optimism, even in the face of failure Organizational commitment	
Empathy	The propensity to suspend judgment – to consider the perspective of others before acting	Expertise in building and retaining talent Cross-cultural sensitivity Service to clients and customers	
Social Skill	An ability to effectively pursue group goals with energy and persistence	Effectiveness in leading change Persuasiveness Expertise in building and leading teams	

Here's a quick look ahead for the remainder of Part I of this book, as we complete the Framework for IT Leadership. In the next chapter, we will review some fundamental concepts from *Picasso on a Schedule* and *Managing Picasso* that are basic to understanding the IT leadership concepts that comprise the heart of this book. In the following chapter, we will begin a more detailed study of leadership proper by introducing and exploring the categories of personal attributes that are most important to effective leadership and effective management. We will see that while leadership and management require the same personal attributes, the order of emphasis of those is different between management and leadership. We will also consider some of the most important basic competencies for excellent leadership, see how these apply to both Hierarchy Leaders and Matrix Leaders, and explore an effective approach that enables individuals to develop their leadership strengths and capabilities.

Chapter 2

Picasso on a Schedule and Managing Picasso: Concepts Review

To delve deeper into the main subject of this book, which focuses on the *Management* and *Leadership* systems of action required in both the Hierarchy and Matrix components of the Hierarchical Matrix Organizational structure, an understanding and working knowledge of some of the major concepts described in our first two books, *Picasso on a Schedule* and *Managing Picasso*, are required.

The IT-OSD Model

In Chapter 1, we briefly introduced a system design model called the Information Technology Organizational System Design Model (IT-OSD Model). In this section we will review this model in more detail.

The IT-OSD Model, which is illustrated again in Figure 2.1:

- Provides an evolutionary and systematic approach to IT organizational design that:
  - Enables the achievement of extraordinary results through the dedicated, but ordinary efforts of people, rather than always looking to heroic efforts from outstanding people to create such results

○ Accomplishes this by giving IT professionals a decision-making framework in which to maintain and support the creativity necessary for excellence, while imposing appropriate structure and controls to ensure a balanced focus on technical and business competence

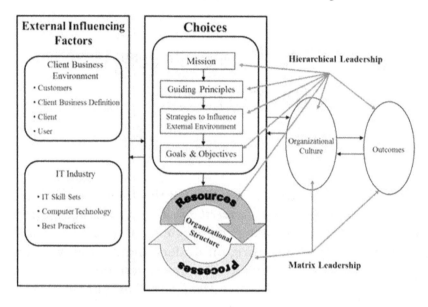

Figure 2.1: *The Information Technology Organizational System Design Model*

There are four major components of the IT-OSD Model:

- The ***External Influencing Factors*** component of the model represents outside elements that directly affect the nature of the results created by an IT organization and are comprised of two broad categories within this component:

  ○ The *Client Business Environment* category is characterized by the following features:

    ▪ It is comprised of the IT organization's clients, the clients' business definitions, their customers, and the users of the systems/services the IT organization delivers

- A client is anyone who purchases IT products or services directly from the IT organization

- The Client Business Environment is defined by the buying and selling of goods and services by the client organization in support of its customers

- The client's customers are the persons or businesses that purchase a commodity or service offered by the client

- A user is any person who uses IT services for activities related to the client's business

○ The *IT Industry* category is characterized by the following features:

- It is comprised of technology providers, the IT staffing marketplace, IT competitors, and IT industry best practices

- Technology providers are the source for computing technology—hardware, software, and communications infrastructure

- The IT staffing marketplace defines the availability of people with the IT skill sets required to support computing technology utilized by the IT organization

- IT competitors are IT companies offering products and services that appeal, or might appeal in the future, to the IT organization's clients

- IT industry best practices offer frameworks in computer systems design, development, maintenance, operations, and management

• The **Choices** component of the model represents a range of important and interrelated organizational *design decisions* that an IT organization must make—some explicit, some implicit—about the following organizational elements:

- ○ Mission

- ○ Guiding Principles

- ○ Major Business Strategies

- ○ Goals and Objectives

- ○ Resources

- ○ Processes

- ○ Organizational Structure

- The *Organizational Culture* component of the model represents the intangible "personality of the organization in action" as articulated in the mission, guiding principles, and strategies. It determines how people are expected to behave most of the time. Culture is characterized by the following features:

  - ○ Culture is formed and changed very slowly over a long period of time, and its development and maintenance requires great effort, skill, and patience

  - ○ Culture that helps *retain good people* is not the same as the staff benefits that helps attract and hire good people

  - ○ "Good" culture can be one of the organization's strengths and competitive advantages

  - ○ "Bad" culture is a great barrier to organizational success

- The *Outcomes* component of the model represents the end results that define the value an organization delivers to its clients. It is imperative that an organization have some tangible qualitative or quantitative measures of achievement of these outcomes to assess its degree of success.

It is the job of the management and leadership teams of an IT organization to oversee the adaption and evolution of the IT-OSD model itself so it can function effectively as a decision-making framework, where we define:

- *Leadership* as a system of action that helps direct, align, and inspire actions on the part of large numbers of people to organize in the first place and to adapt for success in significantly changing circumstances

- *Management* as a system of action that produce a degree of predictability and order through a set of processes that can keep a complicated system of resources (people and technology) running smoothly

- As a consequence of these definitions:

  o The culture and the vision necessary to create and maintain the organization's mission, guiding principles, and strategies will tend to be more in the province of the *Leadership* system of action

  o Overseeing structure and processes and the outcomes these produce will tend to be more the province of the *Management* system of action

The Hierarchical Matrix

As noted, our answer to one of the major choices identified in the IT-OSD Model concerning the design of an organizational structure is a structure called the *Hierarchical Matrix*. In the following paragraphs, we review some of this structure's high-level features.

The Hierarchical Matrix is composed of the following elements:

- **Resources.** The Hierarchical Matrix includes the following three major IT resources:

  1. **Infrastructure**–The underlying base or foundation (i.e. computing platforms, networks, operating systems, enabling software) required to implement and operate Application Systems

2. **Application Systems**–A group of interacting, interrelated, or interdependent computer programs designed for a specific business task or use

3. **People**–Skilled IT personnel

- **Processes.** The Hierarchical Matrix also includes three major categories of integrated, fully developed, repeatable mission-critical processes focused on:

1. The activities that enable the technical workforce to get the work done:

   ▪ The technical workforce and its related processes are collectively referred to as the **Matrix** within the Hierarchical Matrix organizational model

2. The activities that produce a degree of predictability and order for an IT organization that support management in successfully running Information Technology as a business:

   ▪ The management workforce and its related processes are collectively referred to as the **Hierarchy** within the Hierarchical Matrix organizational model

3. The activities focused on the adaptive change of the previously two identified processes:

   ▪ The workforce and processes responsible for adaptive change are collectively referred to as **Governance** within the Hierarchical Matrix organizational model

- **Organizational Structure.** The organizational structure within the Hierarchical Matrix is defined using the **system architecture** as a guide to identify and assign responsibility to organizational units to efficiently acquire and maintain all or some portion of the Infrastructure IT Resources and all or some portion of the Application Systems IT Resources, as follows:

   ○ Each organizational unit is assigned people resources that are responsible for or are participants in all or

some portion of the highly defined repeatable processes required to support the Infrastructure IT Resources
and/or Application Systems IT Resources for which it is
responsible

- ○ The number of people resources assigned to a given IT
  organizational unit is based on the level at which the
  repeatable processes are implemented within the unit
  and scaled appropriately to the IT organization's overall
  mission

The Hierarchical Matrix's **defining characteristics** are:

- It is based on a *specialization strategy* that is realized through
  an interconnected set of basic IT Roles, developed using
  the following guidelines:

  - ○ The processes of the Hierarchical Matrix are created
    with the recognition that the more people specialize,
    the more interdependent they become

  - ○ Each repeatable process is designed to provide the free-
    dom for each person to seek the help they need from
    others to be successful

  - ○ To use this freedom wisely, those in the Hierarchical
    Matrix must understand how their role interrelates with
    other roles and the responsibilities incumbent upon
    those in each role

  - ○ A crucial point is that for individuals working within
    the Hierarchy to be successful, they *must* have a working
    knowledge of both the Hierarchy and Matrix processes

- The success of the Hierarchical Matrix in attaining the
  competing goals of efficiency and effectiveness lies within
  the self-correcting mechanisms of its processes which create a natural equilibrium by:

  - ○ Allowing an IT business to achieve *efficiency* by operat-
    ing as a resource-scarce organization

o At the same time allowing the IT business to achieve *effectiveness* by producing solutions for its clients as if it were a resource-rich organization

o Improving the day-to-day decision-making by purposely designing into each repeatable process self-correction procedures to resolve most work issues within the Matrix without the need for intervention from the Hierarchy

- An *adaptation strategy* was utilized in the creation and organization of the framework of Hierarchical Matrix processes by following these guidelines:

  o Adapt selected IT industry best-practices to the IT organization's needs and culture to complete the definition of the integrated process framework for the organization's administration and operations

  o In applying this strategy, it is important to remember that all IT industry best-practice frameworks are independent, have overlapping components, and have strengths and weaknesses

  o Thus, by choosing components of the various frameworks, rather than adopt one or more frameworks as a whole, an organization is better able to achieve a comprehensive complete process framework

  o The following describes the best-practice frameworks used in the I/S Division's adaptation process:

    ▪ The **Information Technology Infrastructure Library (ITIL)** is a framework of internationally defined best practices for IT service management and support developed by the government of the United Kingdom and published by the IT Service Management Forum. This is a comprehensive IT framework that focuses on *IT service and infrastructure management.*

- The **Capability Maturity Model Integration (CMMI)**, developed by the Software Engineering Institute, is a model for process improvement described in terms of best practices within a framework. This framework focuses on *IT project management and application software engineering.*

- **Control Objectives for Information and related Technology (COBIT)** is an open standard and framework of controls and best practices for IT governance. It is published by the IT Governance Institute (ITGI), a not-for-profit research organization affiliated with the Information Systems Audit and Control Association. This framework focuses on *IT governance and management controls.*

- The **Enterprise Architecture Maturity Model (EAMM)** was developed by the National Association of State Chief Information Officers (NASCIO). It is a model for *system architecture process improvement.*

Guided by these best-practice frameworks for various aspects of the IT industry, we have identified Nine Major Processes which can be thought of as belonging to one of three categories or process groups which are collectively referred to as *The Hierarchical Matrix Process Framework* (or *Rainbow Chart of Processes* for short):

- A category of processes referred to as the ***Adaptive Change* process group** is concerned with optimizing organizational change and monitoring and controlling the other processes to ensure the overall quality necessary for the long-term success of the organization. (Note: it utilizes the IT-OSD Model as an underlying decision-making framework for its processes.)

- A second category referred to as the ***Business Perspective* process group** (or the *Hierarchy* for short) is focused on building and maintaining the necessary client relationships, ensuring the effectiveness of the supporting basic business functions such as planning and budgeting, financial and cost accounting, resource acquisition, contract management, and marketing, as well as defining a complete system of acquisition, care, and treatment of IT human resources.

- The third category referred to as the *System Factory* **process group** (or the *Matrix* for short) comprises the set of processes needed to manage the production of the products and services required by the organization's clients.

- The Three Process Groups and the Nine Major Processes comprise a *complete framework* of all the required major processes for any IT organization as given in Table 2.1:

  ○ Note that in addition to the Nine Major Processes, in Table 2.1 we have shown some sub-processes that might typically be required in order to implement these processes at the next lower level

  ○ Within the Nine Major Processes there is flexibility to allow an IT organization to refine this framework:

    ▪ According to different areas of emphasis appropriate to the nature and structure of its own unique business

    ▪ With the specific sub-processes that are useful for their individual environments as determined by a particular IT organization's mission, strategies, and required outcomes

Table 2.1

Fundamental IT Processes and Process Groups
with Example First-Level Refinements

IT Process Framework

Adaptive Change Process Group

1. **Adaptive Change**
   - IT Governance
   - Quality Assurance

Business Perspective Process Group (The Hierarchy)

2. **Line of Business Management**
   - Financial Management
   - Resource Acquisition
3. **Enabling Processes**
   - Managing People Program
   - Administrative tasks
4. **Client Management**
   - Relationship Management
   - Steering Support (Client Work requests)
   - Product Improvement
   - Systems/Service Monitoring
   - Internal Marketing

System Factory Process Group (The Matrix)

5. **System Architecture**
   - Application Systems Architecture
   - ICT Infrastructure Architecture
6. **Application Systems Management**
   - Project Management
   - Research and Development
   - Application System Development and Maintenance
   - Application System Support
7. **Service Management**
   - Service Support
   - Service Delivery
8. **ICT Infrastructure Management**
   - Infrastructure Deployment Management
   - Operations Management
   - Technical support
9. **Security and Audit Management**
   - Information Security Management
   - Audit Management

Figure 2.2 illustrates an example of a more fully refined Rainbow Chart of Processes that:

- Represents the combined results of the refinement process completed by the I/S Division over the past 20 years, as the organization successfully transitioned from a company of 300 employees processing 700 million online transactions annually, to one of more than 2,000 employees processing over 20 billion online transactions annually

- Represents process refinements that were made over this time frame and that were driven by the nature of the organization's work—developing its own software within an integrated system architecture and running that software for its clients on its own ICT infrastructure.

- Contains the Nine Major Processes, grouped into the Three Process Groups, with sub-process refinements included that are appropriate for an organization that writes its own software, provides its own infrastructure, and makes available applications and data storage within that infrastructure to its clients and their customers

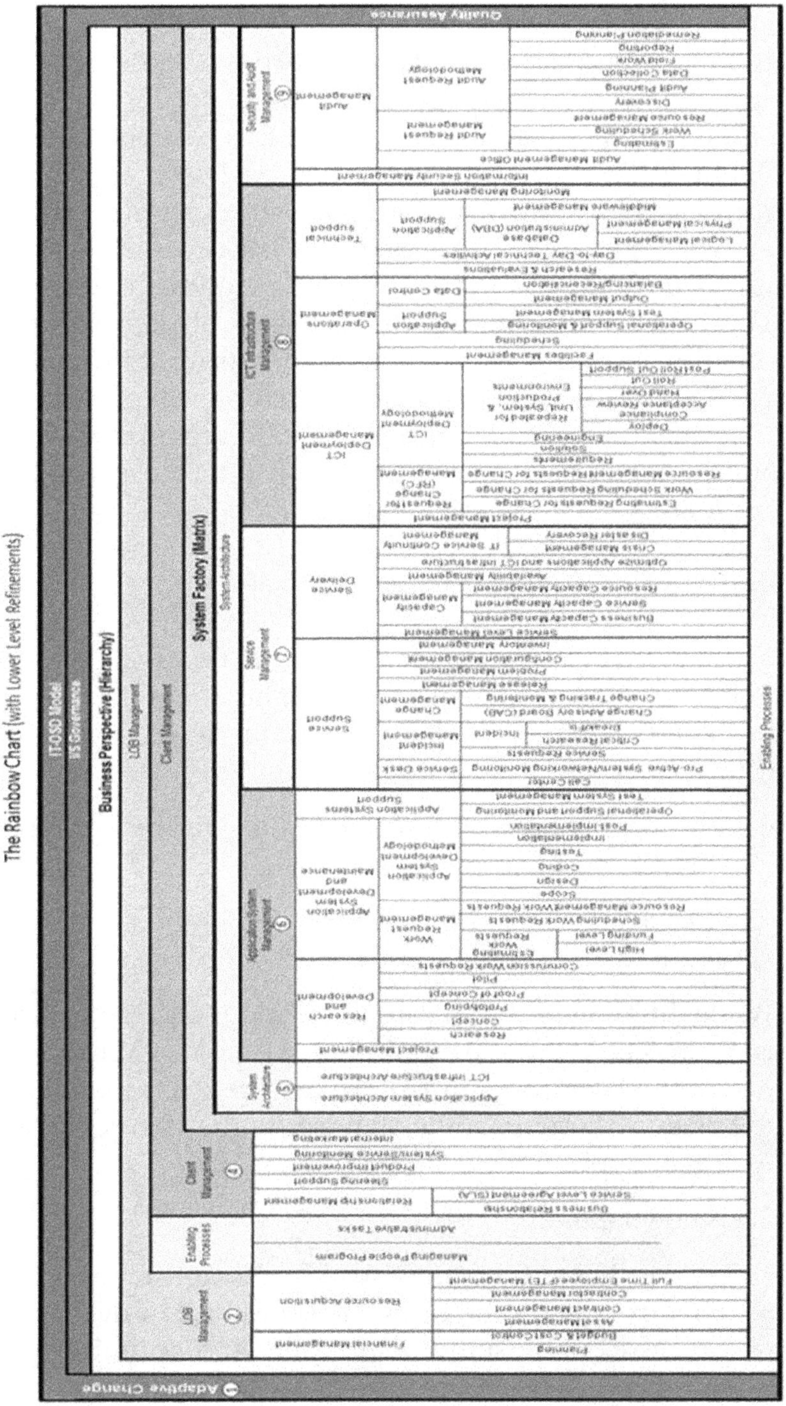

Figure 2.2: *The I/S Division Matrix (as of December 2014) with Lower-level Refinements*

Running IT as a Business

Running IT as a business is the key to meeting the challenge of fulfilling customer value expectations relative to the objectives of cost, time, and quality. Indeed, to run IT as a successful business, the Hierarchy must *balance those three competing objectives.* To accomplish this balancing act, the Hierarchy must meet the *IT Value Challenge* of ensuring that available resources are used as efficiently as possible, of focusing on the technical competence of the IT staff and ensuring the effectiveness of processes that lead to quality outcomes, and of completing its work in a timely manner. When this is done, the IT organization will provide the vital IT systems that enable and support the organization's clients' abilities to compete, and will position the IT organization for future success.

In order to run IT as a successful business:

- The entire organization must maintain focus on the need to balance cost (efficiency) and quality (effectiveness) to meet the challenge of delivering value to its customers, where:

  ○ The precise interpretation of value will be customer-specific

  ○ All customers will have defined their own expectations about the balance of these factors

- While different IT organizations' missions may modify who is responsible for the execution of the various Matrix processes, the Hierarchy must always assume the responsibility to possess a thorough understanding of the Matrix processes as they apply to their organization

- Such understanding:

  ○ Is the basis for effective IT management as the Hierarchy helps the individuals involved in the Matrix processes understand, appreciate, and optimize their interactions

- ○ Must include how these processes relate to the mixture of the major factors of cost, schedule, and quality as measured by the extent to which solution outcomes fulfill customer requirements

The Hierarchy:

- Is ultimately responsible for *balancing three competing objectives: cost, time, and quality* in order to meet the IT Value Challenge of:
  - ○ Ensuring that available resources are used as efficiently as possible
  - ○ Focusing on the technical competence of the IT staff
  - ○ Ensuring the effectiveness of processes that lead to quality outcomes, and of completing its work in a timely manner
- Must impose balance to prevent even the most technically excellent Matrix from falling short on meeting the IT Value Challenge because:
  - ○ Technical professionals in the Matrix will gravitate naturally toward a focus on the achievement of excellence in the products and services that the organization delivers
  - ○ Without appropriate constraints and guidance from the Hierarchy, these same technical professionals will generally fall short in ensuring the focus on best business practices that is necessary to achieve the delicate balance between effectiveness and efficiency which clients will ultimately demand
- Must meet its twofold mission to:
  - ○ Ensure that the current technical work gets done well, by:
    - ▪ Securing, developing, and managing a workforce with the high level of client business knowledge and

technical competence necessary for the organization to provide the outcomes of excellent and innovative products and services to its clients

o Ensure that the organization will be positioned to deliver winning client solutions in the future, by:

- Running IT as a profitable business—or at the least as a zero-cost business within a business—to enable the organization's future success

- Developing an agile and able workforce possessing the creativity and adaptability to meet the business needs of the future

• Must possess two fundamental competencies:

o The *technical competence* to deal with the creative and open-ended nature of IT work coupled with the peculiar nature of software itself

o An *excellent working knowledge of the common business practices and governance* that other non-IT businesses operate under

o Draw on this combined technical and business knowledge because decisions made by the Hierarchy—some explicit, some implicit—will vary between:

- Business decisions identified within the IT-OSD Model

- Technical decisions that will require a deep knowledge of the Matrix technical processes that are used to produce the product and service outcomes that clients depend on

The *Business Perspective* process group within the IT Process Framework described earlier (see Table 2.1 and Figure 2.2) is a set of highly integrated, repeatable, scalable, and complete processes that:

- The Hierarchy can utilize to supply the appropriate amount of management direction and controls to produce a degree of predictability and order in fulfilling customer expectations

- Is highly dependent on the combination of technical and business knowledge we noted earlier

- Contains the three high-level processes: *Line of Business Management, Client Management,* and *Enabling Processes*

Line of Business (LOB) Management

The *Line of Business (LOB) Management* process is focused primarily on ensuring that the IT organization's products and services are provided in a cost-effective manner to its clients. To accomplish this, the Hierarchy must:

- Focus on its responsibilities in assuring the successful execution of the *business of IT*

- Ensure that all areas within an IT organization are held financially accountable by the appropriate LOB managers for any costs charged directly or indirectly to clients

- Have and apply a working knowledge of the common business practices and governance under which successful non-IT businesses operate, such as:

  ○ Business practices within a *Financial Management* sub-process which focuses on finance, cost accounting, contract management, and asset management

  ○ Business practices within a *Planning* sub-process which focuses on work planning and budgeting in order to promote the wise and cost-effective use of IT resources in the pursuit of client business goals

  ○ Business practices within a *Resource Acquisition* sub-process which focuses on obtaining the required IT

Resources within the following three main categories of IT Resources:

- *Application Systems* which refers to a group of inter-acting, interrelated, or interdependent computer programs designed for a specific business task or use

- *Technical infrastructure* which refers to the foundation of computing platforms, networks, operating systems, and enabling software, that are required to implement and operate the various application systems

- IT *people resource* which refers to the group of skilled IT personnel to build or assemble and then maintain the application systems and technical infrastructure

- Properly manage all resources which requires an understanding of the system architecture for the management of application systems and technical infrastructure consistent with and supportive of the IT organization's overall mission

Enabling Processes: Managing People

As a service organization, an IT organization's most important resource is *its people*. Hence the success of the organization will depend to a large extent on how well the organization manages its people. We believe that this can best be accomplished using a set of repeatable processes specifically designed for this purpose, as follows:

- A comprehensive system is required to manage the IT organization's people

- The system must be comprised of the general processes, programs, and information sources that are required to effectively managing the technical staff—both full-time employees (FTE) and contractors

- Figure 2.3 illustrates such a comprehensive system—the *Managing People Program*

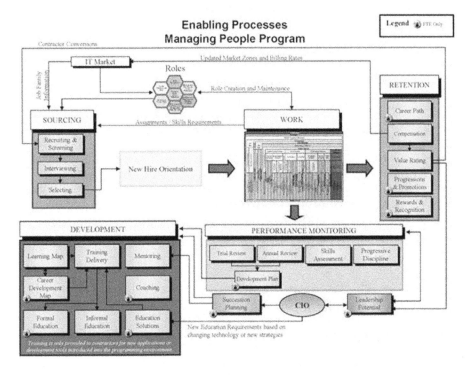

Figure 2.3: *Overview of the Managing People Program*

Client Management

A successful IT organization must cultivate strategic client partnerships through a process referred to as *Client Management*. These partnerships can be established and maintained by utilizing the following strategies:

- Pursuing IT solutions and not just products; effectively focusing IT organization resources on client needs and priorities

- Recognizing that the high value a client places on the quality of the interactions with their product and service suppliers is the differentiator in deciding between suppliers with similar offerings

- Implementing a *client-centric strategy*, which comprises three important principles:

   o Client strategic alignment, which:

      ▪ Aligns the IT organization's resources and initiatives to support the client's strategic initiatives

   o Client focus, which:

      ▪ Allows the client organization to focus on what it knows best—succeeding in its own business environment

      ▪ Permits the IT organization to focus on its expertise in providing outstanding IT solutions that are appropriate and cost-effective for the client's business needs

      ▪ Is based on the development of mutual trust within the client relationship

   o Client control of priorities, which:

      ▪ Works with client strategic alignment to maintain client control of its IT spending priorities

The three Business Perspective processes of LOB Management, the Managing People Program, and Client Management lay the foundation for running IT as a successful business. The additional important factor that is needed to ensure that the organization achieves this outcome is developing great leadership—in both the Hierarchy and the Matrix.

Chapter 3

Fundamentals of Leadership Development

The more great leaders an organization develops, the more it will become an outstanding organization. There is no reason to accept mediocrity in leadership any more than in software programming, customer service, or selling.

Jack Zenger and Joseph Folkman
From The Extraordinary Leader

Great leadership is an essential and driving force for the success of any organization. And as we have earlier noted, leadership in the IT setting surely involves a blending of art and science. However, it is clear that defining great leadership in a precise and scientific way is a difficult if not impossible challenge. The multitude and popularity of books on leadership reflects both on how varied are opinions about what constitutes great leadership, as well as how intrigued we are to uncover the "secrets" of great leadership. Many of these books focus on identifying people who have been recognized and acclaimed as great leaders, and then attempting to abstract those qualities of character and temperament that have contributed to their success as leaders. Inherent in all these attempts to capture the essence of great leadership is this fundamental question: *Are great leaders born or made?*

Is there a relatively small cadre of people in the world who are "great leaders in waiting" who simply need the right opportunities to demonstrate their exemplary leadership abilities? Or, are the underlying characteristics that make great leaders present in a larger group of talented people who could in fact be developed into great leaders? We believe that the answer to this question of whether leaders are born or made is—*both*. And this answer has important impact for organizations as they strive to find the leadership that they realize is so important to their ultimate success.

Studies have shown there is some predisposition for and genetic influence on leadership potential, and thus there is an obvious need for organizations to put serious effort into a selection process to find its best *potential leaders*. However, those same studies also show that 2/3 of leadership strengths are strongly influenced by one's environment. [4] As a consequence, we believe that leaders can be made rather than born because leadership strengths are skills and behaviors that can be developed. Of course, to do this successfully, careful attention must be given to ensure that those to be developed in this way have in fact demonstrated some innate potential for leadership.

Personal Attributes for Effective Leadership

Over the years, the I/S Division of BlueCross BlueShield of South Carolina has identified a set of key management and leadership personal attributes that have proved particularly important in the success of that organization. These key personal attributes are distributed over four categories: People Management, Process Management, Personal Characteristics, and Strategic Management. These categories of personal attributes are important for both effective leadership and effective management, but studies [3] have shown that the order of emphasis is different for management and leadership. For effective leadership, the order of emphasis on Strategic Management and Process Management is flipped from the order of emphasis of these two in effective management. This is illustrated in Figure 3.1.

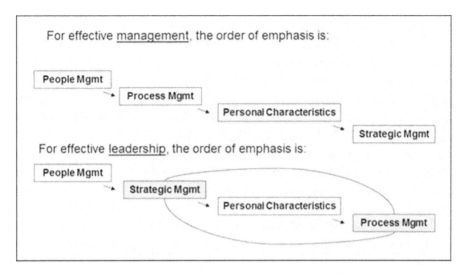

Figure 3.1: *Order of Importance of Key Attribute Categories for Leadership and Management.*

The key attributes within these categories are shown in Table 3.1, with attributes that have been shown in our experience to be particularly important to *effective leadership* shaded.

Table 3.1: *The I/S Division's Effective Leadership and Management Key Personal Attributes.*

People Management	Personal Characteristics	Process Management	Strategic Management
Clearly communicate expectations	Accept responsibility for success and failures	Appropriately handle crises	Adapt to changing circumstances
Correctly evaluate potential in others	Challenge the status quo	Break down a project into manageable components	Correctly assess the risk and return of decisions
Hold people accountable	Comfortable with ambiguity	Correctly allocate resources across competing priorities	Deep understanding of markets, competitors and customers

Inspire others	Committed to continuous personal development	Create clear work plans and timetables	Global perspective
Persuade and encourage others to move in a desired direction	Confident	Creatively solve problems	Identify and articulate long-term vision for future
Put the right people in the right roles at the right time	Honesty and Integrity	Encourage and manage innovation	Properly manage relationships with third parties
Recognize and reward achievement	Intelligent	Measure results	Understanding strengths and weaknesses of company
Strong commitment to diversity	Negotiate effectively	Properly manage budgets and timelines	
Strong commitment to development	Open to new ideas	Translate a long-term vision into a step-by-step plan	
	Original		
	Passion to succeed		
	Perseverance		
	Influential		
	Sensitive to others' needs		
	Decisive		
	Think analytically		
	Years of management experience		

Differentiating Competencies for Effective Leadership

Based on in-depth studies of data collected on successful leaders across many different businesses, Jack Zenger and Joseph Folkman [4] have identified 19 strengths (behaviors and traits) that distinguish exceptional leaders, and that can be used to guide the development of effective leaders. Zenger and Folkman refer to these as *differentiating competencies* and they fall into five categories as follows:

Character

   1. Displays High Integrity and Honesty

Personal Capability

   2. Strategic Technical Leadership

   3. Issues Resolution

   4. Innovates

   5. Practices Self-Discipline

   6. Decision-Making

Focuses on Results

   7. Drives for Results

   8. Establishes Stretch Goals

   9. Takes Initiative

  10. Resource Planning and Management

Interpersonal Skills

  11. Organizational Leadership/Communication

  12. Coaching/Inspiring Others

  13. Business Relationships

  14. People Process Management/Staff Development

  15. Flexibility/Collaboration/Teamwork

  16. Delegation

Leading Change

  17. Strategic Thinking

  18. Managing Change

  19. Connects the Group to the Outside World

Table 3.2: I/S Leadership/Management Attributes Cross-Referenced to Differentiating Competencies.

People Management (11)	Personal Characteristics (1)	Process Management (7, 9)	Strategic Management (2, 15)
Clearly communicate expectations (10, 14)	Accept responsibility for success and failures (18)	Appropriately handle crises (3, 9, 16)	Adapt to changing circumstances (6, 18)
Correctly evaluate potential in others (8, 12, 14)	Challenge the status quo (4, 15)	Break down a project into manageable components (10, 16)	Correctly assess the risk and return of decisions (2, 6)
Hold people accountable (7, 12)	Comfortable with ambiguity (5, 18)	Correctly allocate resources w/ competing priorities (10, 16)	Deep understanding of markets, competitors and customers (19)
Inspire others (12)	Committed to continuous personal development (9)	Create clear work plans and timetables (3, 7)	Global perspective (17)
Persuade and encourage others to move in a desired direction (8, 10)	Confident (1, 9)	Creatively solve problems (4)	Identify and articulate long-term vision for future (13, 17, 19)
Put the right people in the right roles at the right time (10, 15)	Honesty and Integrity (1)	Encourage and manage innovation (8, 15)	Properly manage relationships with third parties (2, 13)
Recognize and reward achievement (14)	Intelligent (3, 6)	Measure results (10)	Understanding strengths/weaknesses of company (17, 19)
Strong commitment to diversity (14)	Negotiate effectively (3, 4)	Properly manage budgets/timelines (17)	
Strong commitment to development (8, 9)	Open to new ideas (2, 4)	Translate a long-term vision into a step-by-step plan (17, 18)	
	Original (4, 7, 8)		

	Passion to succeed **(7, 12)**		
	Perseverance **(3, 5, 12)**		
	Influential **(13, 17)**		
	Sensitive to the needs of others **(6, 12)**		
	Decisive **(3, 9)**		
	Think analytically **(2)**		
	Years of experience in positions of management		

As illustrated in Table 3.2, the I/S Division's leadership and management key personal attributes can be cross-referenced to the set of differentiating competencies identified in the study by Zenger and Folkman. In the table the cross references are identified using the numbering (1-19) of the differentiating competencies given above. It is interesting to note that each of the 19 differentiating competencies is cross-referenced to at least one key attribute, and that many of the key attributes are cross-referenced to multiple differentiating competencies. These interconnections suggest a high correlation between the two leadership models for an IT organization.

Leadership Development for Organizational Success

So the question becomes: "Can effective Hierarchy and Matrix Leaders use these insights about key attributes and differentiating competencies to develop their leadership capacities and significantly increase their positive impact on their organizations?" As suggested by our earlier comments about whether leaders are born or made, we believe the answer to this question is a resounding "Yes!"

For an organization to set the context for the kind of leadership development that will dramatically impact its success, we believe it should embrace two fundamental principles that form the foundation of an effective approach to organizational leadership development:

1. **Do Not Expect Perfection.** No one is perfect and leaders are no exception. History demonstrates very clearly that even the most effective leaders have both strengths and weaknesses.

2. **Develop Strengths for Dramatic Organizational Impact.** Great leaders invariably demonstrate exceptional strengths in one or more dimensions that make a difference to their organizations. The best approach for personal leadership development is to discover which of your strengths best fit with the needs and aspirations of the organization, then work to make those strengths exceptional.

A person wishing to develop his or her leadership is faced with a number of important questions, including:

- What are my strengths and weaknesses as a leader?

- Which of these strengths and weaknesses should I focus on?

- What progress should I expect and how will I measure it?

- How important is leadership development relative to my other more immediate responsibilities?

- How can I optimize my leadership development efforts within my organizational context?

As we will see, the two fundamental principles given above help provide answers to these important questions that enable a person to plan and execute an effective leadership development course of action.

Discover Your Leadership Strengths and Weaknesses

As we have discussed, leadership is not an easily defined entity. It involves a complex and subtle combination of personal characteristics, attitudes, behaviors, skills, and abilities. But because the impact of leadership is clearly reflected in how well the leader is able to inspire and persuade others to follow, the *perception* of all these attributes is of paramount importance. Hence an effective approach to begin the assessment of our leadership skills is to make efforts to discover the perception that others have of us as leaders.

To use this approach successfully, we must overcome our human nature tendency to be defensive when others offer their views of our strengths and weaknesses. While it is true that others' perceptions of us may not reflect who we truly are in every case, we have to accept the fact that in the realm of leadership—which can be effective only if others follow—perceptions are in fact their own reality. So to become a more effective leader, we must be willing to accept these perceptions from others and learn from them.

There are several ways in which we can begin to understand how our leadership is being perceived. Most directly, we should always be open to, and in fact ask for, feedback within the context of our day-to-day work. In so doing, we should encourage honest feedback and not react badly when this honesty is less complimentary than we would have hoped it would be. Feedback should be solicited from those we work for, those who report to us, and others that we work with in various capacities.

A more organized way to seek feedback on specific characteristics is to utilize a survey instrument. The 360-degree survey concept can be very useful as it allows us to collect feedback on a set of common factors from a number of sources who see us from different perspectives. The research data supporting the analysis we cited earlier on differentiating competencies by Zenger and Folkman is based on thousands of responses utilizing such a survey instrument.

It is important to realize that feedback will be of little use unless we couple it with honest introspection. So, however we obtain this kind of feedback, we must be disciplined enough to look at ourselves and our behaviors honestly, recognizing and accepting that these behaviors may not always accurately reflect our intentions. On the other hand, we must not overreact and see every negative feedback data point as a mandate for change. Balance is the key—the goal is to consider the aggregate feedback and gain an *overall assessment* about the perceptions others with whom we work have of our strengths and weaknesses as leaders.

Strive for the Right Balance

Once we have some data that informs us about others' perceptions of our strengths and weaknesses, what next? Our first principle points the way: *Do Not Expect Perfection.* It is a natural human tendency to focus on the perceptions about our weaknesses. While we don't want to ignore those, putting too much emphasis on those can prevent us from reaching our goal to become a great leader. As we noted earlier, history teaches us that all great leaders have both strengths and weaknesses. Examples abound, but we will cite just two cases that illustrate our point, namely Generals George Patton and Douglas MacArthur—two of the most successful American battlefield leaders of World War II. Both these leaders had exemplary strengths.

General George Patton was able to motivate his troops to remarkable levels of achievement. He led the US Seventh Army in a highly successful and rapid drive in the Sicily invasion, and his armored drive across France with the US Third Army was a major factor in the final Allied victory in Europe. Yet his success as a commander was at times overshadowed by his proclivity to make controversial public statements which were at odds with American foreign policy. General Dwight Eisenhower struggled to manage Patton's great strengths and at the same time protect him from himself and try to minimize the damage he was doing to the often delicate US alliance with Britain and Russia which was critical to the overall success of the war effort.

Similarly, General Douglas MacArthur could inspire troops to achieve great successes and he demonstrated extraordinary vision in adopting an island hopping strategy in the Pacific which was a key factor in the successful campaign against Japan, resulting in victory with significantly reduced casualties. Following Japan's surrender, he served admirably as a military governor of Japan, following a wise pragmatic strategy that helped enable Japan to make stunning economic, political and social changes that fueled its recovery from a state of almost total collapse at the end of the war. And later, with his surprise landing at Inchon in Korea, he turned near defeat into a stunning reversal of fortunes in the Korean Conflict. Yet MacArthur was a shameless self-promoter who was paranoid and distrustful even of his own staff. He demanded excessive loyalty from subordinates and this characteristic led him to often choose less capable people to fill those roles. His arrogance led him to display a tendency toward defiance and obstinacy, including his disobedience of President Hoover's orders during the veterans' riots in Washington, D.C., and culminating in President Truman relieving him of command over his defiance about American policy in Korea.

The lesson to be drawn from these examples is that extraordinary strengths can allow a person to exert great leadership in spite of the presence of serious flaws. However, if the flaws are too great, the ultimate result can be less than optimal achievement and even failure. As a consequence, the person who aspires to great leadership should do two things:

- Develop existing strengths to become extraordinary
- Ensure that major flaws are controlled so that these are not allowed to overshadow strengths and reduce the potential positive impact of leadership

Develop Your Profound Strengths

In the study that we referenced earlier, Zenger and Folkman refer to the leadership strengths that other people perceive as clearly outstanding as potential *profound strengths.* They assert, and we agree, that to be a great leader the leader must develop such strengths to the level that enable extraordinary contributions to the organization. Indeed this is the basis of our second fundamental principle: *Develop Strengths for Dramatic Organizational Impact.* In other words, instead of trying to improve across the board in all competencies, the approach should be to work diligently on those things you're already good at and focus on becoming even better at them.

The reason for this approach is that, as demonstrated by the Zenger and Folkman research, the impact a leader has on organizational success is not primarily a function of *the number* of strengths they possess, but rather results from the *profound strengths they possess.* An attempt to improve in all areas is likely to produce a higher "average leadership competency," but it will likely deter from building profound strengths in a smaller number of areas.

The positive impact of increasing competency in an area is not linear, but grows exponentially as the competency moves into the extraordinary range (90th percentile and up). Leaders with 3 to 5 profound strengths at the 90th percentile in comparison with rankings for other leaders make the highest contributions to an organization for one and only one reason: *They do a few things exceptionally well!*

Remedy Fatal Flaws

So in developing profound strengths, should a person ignore his or her leadership weaknesses? The surprising answer is "yes," except in some special cases. Those special cases are when a weakness is so large that it prevents the attainment of the potentially dramatic positive impacts of even profound strengths. Zenger and Folkman dub such weaknesses as *fatal flaws.* In short, a fatal flaws is a trait or competency that is a profound weakness and that is both important on the job and readily observed by others. When such a flaw is discovered, then it absolutely must be "remedied" before the leader can increase his or her positive impact on the organization.

However remedying a fatal flaw does not mean working on the flaw with the goal of turning it into a great strength. First of all this is unlikely to even be possible. And even if it were, the energy and effort it would take would not likely pay commensurate dividends for the individual or the organization, because in achieving this, a person would no doubt be neglecting the further development of potentially profound strengths that they already possess.

The Pathway to Success

The bottom line is this. Work on any fatal flaws to get them up to an "average" level, so that they will no longer stand in your way of become an extraordinary leader. However, remember that fixing a 'fatal flaw' will only get the leader back to ground zero, but does not elevate the leader. Once you have achieved a remedy, focus on developing your potentially profound strengths, because it will be these strengths that move your career and the organization forward.

In summary, the best pathway to becoming an exceptional leader is based on the following observations:

- Focus on developing existing leadership strengths into profound strengths (defined in the Zenger and Folkman study as 90th percentile comparison with rankings for other leaders)
  - Fixing weaknesses has never made anyone exceptional, but developing strengths can
  - The Zenger and Folkman research shows that:
    - Only 28% of leaders have a fatal flaw, and those people should focus on remedying any such flaws first

- The remaining 72% of leaders should focus on building profound strengths

- *Motivation* is increased when a person is working on something they enjoy—a potential strength—thus they invest more time and effort into improvement

- A person is likely to be *more successful* in their change efforts related to developing their strengths (as opposed to focusing on weaknesses), because these strengths have the potential to substantially increase their overall leadership effectiveness

- As a person *sees changes* in outcomes when they focus their development on strengths, this provides incentive and motivation for further development

Leadership Competencies for the Matrix and the Hierarchy

All but three of the 19 differentiating competencies cited earlier apply to both Matrix Leaders and Hierarchy Leaders. However, some are interpreted somewhat differently depending on the type of leadership being considered. Table 3.3 illustrates with those competencies which are different for Matrix Leader shown in italics. In addition, when developed into profound strengths the five shaded competencies have the biggest organizational impact.

Table 3.3: Differentiating Competencies for Hierarchy and Matrix Leaders

	Hierarchy Leader	Matrix Leader			Hierarchy Leader	Matrix Leader
1	Displays High Integrity and Honesty	Displays High Integrity and Honesty		11	Organizational Leadership/ Communication	*Communicates Powerfully and Prolifically*
2	Strategic Technical Leadership	*Technical/ Professional Expertise*		12	Coaching/ Inspiring Others	*Inspires Others to High Performance*
3	Issues Resolution	*Solves Problems/ Analyzes Issues*		13	Business Relationships	Builds Relationships

	Hierarchy Leader	Matrix Leader			Hierarchy Leader	Matrix Leader
4	Innovates	Innovates		14	People Process Management/ Staff Development	*Develops Others*
5	Practices Self-Development	Practices Self-Development		15	Flexibility/ Collaboration/ Teamwork	*Collaboration/ Teamwork*
6	Decision Making	N/A		16	Delegation	N/A
7	Drives for Results	Drives for Results		17	Strategic Thinking	*Broad Perspective*
8	Establishes Stretch Goals	Establishes Stretch Goals		18	Managing Change	*Supports Change*
9	Takes Initiative	Takes Initiative		19	Connects the Group to the Outside World	Connects the Group to the Outside World
10	Resource Planning and Management	N/A				

Behaviors Associated with the Top Five Competencies

It is instructive to consider in more detail the types of behaviors that characterize the five competencies that have the biggest organizational impact. Of these five competencies, four have slightly different meanings in the Hierarchy and the Matrix. For all the competencies, Hierarchy and Matrix Leaders will share many behaviors, but a few of the behaviors will apply only to Hierarchy Leaders. Where this is the case, those behaviors are marked with an asterisk.

- *Behaviors Characterizing Differentiating Competency # 3*

  Issues Resolution (Hierarchy Leader)

  Solves Problems and Analyzes Issues (Matrix Leader)

  ○ Collects data from multiple sources when solving a problem

- Asks the right questions to obtain the information needed to size up a situation properly

- Obtains accurate and crucial information as a basis for sound organization-wide decisions

- Systematically evaluates information by using a variety of proven methods and techniques

- Encourages alternative approaches and new ideas

- Encourages others to seek and try different approaches for solving complex problems

- Sees patterns and trends in complex data and uses the patterns to outline a path forward

- Coaches others on how to analyze information to solve problems and make decisions*

- Clarifies complex data or situations so that others can comprehend, respond and contribute*

- Proactively shares data with others to help them analyze situations*

- *Behaviors Characterizing Differentiating Competency # 8*

Establishes Stretch Goals (Hierarchy and Matrix Leaders)

- Generates agreement among group members on achieving aggressive goals

- Builds commitment with all employees on team goals and objectives*

- Fosters the confidence of others that goals will be achieved

- Promotes a spirit of continuous improvement

- Maintains high standards of performance

- o Sets measurable standards of excellence for self and others in the work group*

- *Behaviors Characterizing Differentiating Competency # 11*

  Organizational Leadership/Communication (Hierarchy Leader)

  Communicates Powerfully and Prolifically (Matrix Leader)

  - o Communicates clearly and concisely
  - o Delivers effective presentations and speeches*
  - o Uses strong writing and verbal skills to communicate facts, figures and ideas to others*
  - o Skillfully communicates new insights
  - o Breaks down communication barriers between teams and departments*

- *Behaviors Characterizing Differentiating Competency # 12*

  Coaching/Inspires Others (Hierarchy Leader)

  Inspires Others to High Performance (Matrix Leader)

  - o Has a personal style that helps to positively motivate others
  - o Energizes people to go the extra mile
  - o Skillfully persuades others toward commitment to ideas or action
  - o Effectively exercises power to influence key decisions for the benefit of the organization*
  - o Employs different motivational strategies to influence the behavior of others*
  - o Inspires others to support organizational priorities

- *Behaviors Characterizing Differentiating Competency # 17*

   Strategic Thinking (Hierarchy Leader)

   Broad Perspective (Matrix Leader)

   - Knows how work relates to the organization's business strategy

   - Balances the short-term and long-term needs of the organization

   - Demonstrates forward thinking about tomorrow's issues

   - Proposes initiatives that become part of the organization's strategic plan*

   - Clarifies vision, mission, values and long-term goals for others*

   - Translates the organization's vision and objectives into challenging and meaningful goals for others

   - Ensures that work group goals are aligned with the organization's strategic goals and vision

   - Explains to others how changes in one part of the organization affect other organizational systems*

   - Sets and articulates a compelling vision for the organization*

   - Continually communicates the highest-priority strategic initiatives to keep the leadership team focused on the right things*

   - Ensures that all systems in the organization are aligned toward achieving the overall strategic goals*

   - Leads organizational efforts that exploit the most highly leveraged business opportunities*

Note that lists of behaviors that characterize *all of the 19 differentiating competencies* are given in the Appendix.

Companion Competencies

In addition to the 19 differentiating competencies, Zenger and Folkman also discovered 46 other competencies, which they called *companion competencies*, that:

- Are skills and behaviors that are statistically correlated with a differentiating competency and when *combined* can accelerate the development of a **profound strength** in that competency

- Opens the door to people's thinking and gives them fresh avenues to pursue when they get stuck in their development of a profound strength

When working on developing a profound strength in a differentiating competency, it is very useful to work on that competency's companion competencies as well, because the Zenger and Folkman research has shown that increasing strength in companion competencies invariably is associated with increasing strength in corresponding differentiating competencies. Therefore, it is instructive to consider the companion competencies for the five differentiating competencies that have the biggest organizational impact. Note that these associations, while proven powerful by the data, do not reflect simple cause and effect relationships. In other words, working on a companion competency does not necessarily cause the differentiating competency to increase. Rather developing the companion competencies along with a differentiating competency allows a person to create a powerful combination of competencies that seem to reinforce each other. In a sense, the whole becomes more than its parts!

- *Companion Competencies for Differentiating Competency # 3*

  Issues Resolution (Hierarchy Leader)

  Solves Problems and Analyzes Issues (Matrix Leader)

  - Ability to Integrate

  - Acts Independently

- ○ Decisiveness
- ○ Desires to Take Challenges
- ○ Innovates
- ○ Planning and Organization
- ○ Takes Initiative
- *Companion Competencies for Differentiating Competency # 8*

  Establishes Stretch Goals (Hierarchy and Matrix Leaders)
  - ○ Decisiveness
  - ○ Drives for Results
  - ○ Gains the Support of Others
  - ○ Sets High Personal Standards
  - ○ Understands Issues
  - ○ Willing to Take Risks and Challenge the Status Quo
- *Companion Competencies for Differentiating Competency # 11*

  Organizational Leadership/Communication (Hierarchy Leader)

  Communicates Powerfully and Prolifically (Matrix Leader)
  - ○ Analytical and Problem-Solving Skills
  - ○ Innovates
  - ○ Involves Others
  - ○ Positive Optimism
  - ○ Takes initiative
  - ○ Translates Messages to Fit
  - ○ Trust

- *Companion Competencies for Differentiating Competency # 12*

  Coaching/Inspires Others (Hierarchy Leader)

  Inspires Others to High Performance (Matrix Leader)
    - Acts as a Role Model in the Organization
    - Adapts Influence Strategies to Individuals
    - Concern and Consideration for Others
    - Creates a Compelling Vision
    - Creates a Learning Environment
    - Empowers Others to Take Responsibility for Projects
    - Ensures Agreement on Priorities
    - Innovates
    - Keeps Team Informed
    - Sets High Personal Standards

- *Companion Competencies for Differentiating Competency # 17*

  Strategic Thinking (Hierarchy Leader)

  Broad Perspective (Matrix Leader)
    - Analytical and Problem-Solving Skills
    - Business Acumen
    - Communication
    - Customer Focus
    - Establishes Stretch Goals
    - Innovates

Why Leadership Matters

One of the most important findings in the Zenger and Folkman research is that leadership provides an essential catalyst for organizational results in two central dimensions:

- Employee Satisfaction and Retention

- Customer Satisfaction

The causal relationship is that leadership effectiveness yields enhanced employee satisfaction which is in turn a major driver of customer satisfaction as illustrated in Figure 3.2.

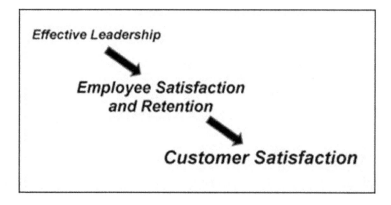

Figure 3.2: *The Impact of Effective Leadership on Organizational Success*

Conventional wisdom attributes employee satisfaction and retention to such 'magic bullet' factors as salary, benefits, status, enhanced working conditions, state-of-the-art equipment, flexible schedules, and availability of childcare. However, in a landmark study conducted over 50 years ago, Herzberg referred to these 'magic bullet' factors as *hygiene factors,* and went on to show that ultimate employee satisfaction and retention actually resides much more in a different set of factors that he called *motivational factors.* Motivational factors include such intangibles as opportunity for achievement, recognition, the work itself, responsibility, advancement, and personal growth. Herzberg's findings have been replicated by many additional research studies over the past half century. [5]

What the Zenger and Folkman research has revealed is that *the additional factor of effective leadership* has a direct and significant impact on the effectiveness of these motivational factors resulting in increased employee satisfaction and hence ultimately increased customer satisfaction. This doesn't minimize the importance of supplying the necessary 'magic bullet' factors, for without these basics, employees will be unhappy. But it is the motivational factors that have the capacity to truly motivate and inspire employees to greater results, and the Zenger and Folkman data demonstrate that effective leadership is an essential underlying factor that pushes these results to higher levels.

More specifically the Zenger and Folkman data showed that:

- Effective leadership explains more variability in employee satisfaction and retention than any of the conventional wisdom 'magic bullet' factors

- Having all the 'magic bullets' makes little difference to employees with a poor leader

- The effectiveness of the leader sets the stage to allow other factors (hygiene and motivational) to be more highly valued

- Similar results are observed for organizations employing 250,000 or 250 people

- Poor leaders receive significantly lower customer satisfaction ratings

- The best leaders receive substantially higher customer satisfaction ratings

The Nonlinear Impact of Effective Leadership

One of the most important findings in the Zenger and Folkman study was that the impact of effective leadership on employee and customer satisfaction is very nonlinear. For example, the study found that leaders who ranked in the bottom 20% of those studied (in 360 degree scores) have a negative impact on both employee and customer satisfaction. Moving from "bad" (lowest 20th percentile) to "good" (30th to 60th) produced significant improvement in both these dimensions. But interestingly, the improvement remained relatively incremental through the middle percentiles (30th to 60th). However the improvement seen when leaders were able to move to the 70th, 80th, and 90th percentiles was much more dramatic. In other words, the same amount of percentile improvement in average 360 degree scores produced far greater results at the upper end of the range of scores.

Not surprisingly, the overall ranking of leadership effectiveness is directly related to the number of perceived profound strengths as Table 3.4 illustrates.

Table 3.4: Overall Leadership Effectiveness and the Number of Profound Strengths

Number of Profound Strengths	0	1	2	3	4	5
Average Percentile Leadership Effectiveness	34	64	72	81	89	91

Note that the dramatic jump in effectiveness when a person moves from 0 to 1 profound strength is a convincing endorsement of the strategy to focus on developing profound strengths instead of a more distributed effort to improve all competencies.

Linear and Nonlinear Development Efforts

Most self-development plans are linear, meaning that they focus on incremental achievement of specific developmental goals and objectives. Such development plans tend to work best for beginners and those correcting weaknesses by encompassing activities that are logical and obvious approaches for an individual to improve.

Linear development efforts comprise three stages:

- Learning the basics

    ○ Skills include proficiency in basic tasks like: conducting a meeting or delegating an assignment

    ○ This learning is through observation of others performing the skills, is casual and informal, and happens at seemingly random times and short bursts

- Learning through formal development

    ○ Skills range from specifics like coaching, mentoring, making effective presentations, delegating wisely, problem solving, and interviewing to broad topics like emotional intelligence, inspiration, or motivation

    ○ This learning can include a process called behavior modeling using video clips showing skills in use and course content explaining the action steps involved and then having participants practicing and rehearsing these skills with one another, using simulations, or working on projects to acquire the skill

- Building in feedback processes

    ○ Used to increase the value of formal development by providing participants with a clearer picture of their abilities through an objective feedback loop

It is important to realize that linear development plans quickly reach a point of diminishing return as the person plateaus by reaching a higher-level of proficiency. This is illustrated by the previously cited Zenger and Folkman finding that leaders who move from "bad" (lowest 20th percentile) to "good" (30th to 60th) see their improvement remain relatively incremental through these middle percentiles (30th to 60th).

On the other hand, non-linear development efforts work best with advanced learners who are reasonably good at an activity and who want to excel at it by encompassing a series of other related activities that help them move into the higher performance ranks of the original activity.

Non-linear development efforts also comprise three stages:

- Doing cross-training
  - This learning involves a process that allows someone who is reasonably good at one of the 19 differentiating competencies to move toward turning this competency into a profound strength
  - Progress in this quest can be accelerated by engaging in a series of activities focused on improvement in one or more companion competencies related to the selected potential profound strength
  - Working on several companion competencies in parallel can help propel a person into the higher performance ranks of the selected potential profound strength
- Learning while working
  - This learning involves a process in which the person in concert with their manager strive to identify opportunities for appropriate development activities that can be integrated into their current position
  - There are two general components to such a process:
    - Action Learning Process. Senior leadership identifies a key problem for an action learning team to solve which is related to the participants' current work using a deliberate, explicit, and planned activity.

- After-Action Review Process. At the conclusion of a given work activity, a facilitated meeting takes place to explore what went well and what could have gone better to answer the key questions about what would be done differently next time.

- Creating sustainability
  - This learning uses a process that requires a Development Plan combined with follow-through activities to lock the desired competency into place
  - The desired sustainability comes from:
    - The learner's motivation and readiness to complete the Development Plan
    - Clarity of the goal which ensures the learner sees the importance of the skill, how it can be applied in the course of their work, and what the skill looks like in practice
    - Support of others which comes from the Culture of the organization and ensures there is a supportive environment from managers, peers, and subordinates for skills development
    - Opportunities for practice using well-defined accountability and responsibility for learners implementing and applying what they learn
    - Continued measurement of progress using a 360 degree feedback instrument
    - Follow-up activities such as working with accountability partners, filing written progress reports, and attending group meetings

Part II
Culture and Leadership

Chapter 4

Build and Nurture Culture

Culture and leadership are two sides of the same coin in that leaders first start the process of culture creation when they create organizations, {but} if they do not become conscious of the cultures in which they are embedded, those cultures will manage them. Cultural understanding is desirable for all of us, but it is essential to leaders if they are to lead.

Edgar Schein

Organizational culture is an abstraction comprising a complex blend of human behavior, attitudes, assumptions, and beliefs. Although an abstraction, culture creates significant tangible impacts; it has the power to energize and mobilize an organization toward great accomplishments, or to shackle it with unproductive and debilitating stagnation. To create a strong energizing culture, an organization must have a clear set of values and norms that guide the way an organization actually operates. Outstanding cultures depend on the organization clearly articulating its vision, mission, values, and goals and then creating systems of action that leverage and resonate with these.

The importance of culture is often misunderstood and it can sometimes be discounted as a "soft" element of a business, promoted by the Human Resources Department, but having little real impact on the organization's focus to perform and achieve. But in reality, culture is one of the most important drivers of long-term, sustainable success. Culture creates the environment in which an organization thrives or dies a slow death.

Culture cannot be created with a checklist of prescribed actions. It has to be genuinely nurtured by everyone within the organization starting at the very top. As Schein has noted "culture and leadership are two sides of the same coin," and it is leadership's responsibility to engage the entire organization in the understanding and nurturing of a culture that will support and inspire those in the organization to achieve its core purposes. [6]

What is Culture?

Whether an organization will, or will not, have a culture is not a matter of choice. Every operational organization has a culture which has an important impact—recognized or unrecognized—on the organization's success. The issue is rather whether the organization will invest the effort to articulate and understand its culture and take an active approach to developing and nurturing it.

Everyone in an organization, through their day-to-day actions as well as their own unique personalities, contributes to the maintenance of the past culture and the evolution of future culture. Therefore, to enable the effective development and nurturing of culture, everyone must embrace the organization's culture, try to understand it, work within it, and help optimize its role in the organization's success.

There are many definitions of organizational culture, but our interpretation of culture is based on Edgar Schein's definition [6]:

The culture of a group can be defined as a pattern of shared basic assumptions learned by a group as it solved its problems of external adaption and internal integration, which has worked well enough to be considered valid and, therefore to be taught to new members as the correct way to perceive, think, and feel in relation to these problems.

In other words, an IT organization's culture is defined as how the *organization behaves*, its essential character as it goes about day-to-day work to produce its prescribed outcomes. Culture comprises the implicit, unwritten rules for getting along in the organization, the way things are done, the "ropes" that every newcomer has to learn to become an accepted and valued member of the group. Culture embodies the shared cognitive frames—mental models, shared meanings, stories about past successes, common understandings, linguistic paradigms—that guide the perceptions, thought, and language used by members of the group and are taught to new members as part of their socialization process.

It is important to note that interpretation of culture is always a personal thing. From an individual's perspective, understanding and embracing organizational culture can mean the difference between being successfully assimilated into an organization or feeling like you are constantly swimming upstream and trying to fit in. In order to be learned, culture must be experienced and then related in the individual's mind to the way the organization does its work.

Though there are tangible and codifiable ways to recognize and assess culture, as we will explore a bit later, the knowledge a person needs to truly understand culture goes well beyond this codifiable base to the kind of tacit knowledge that can come only from one's own experiences and from the advice and guidance of trusted and more experienced members of the organization. Indeed, one of the most important benefits of the IT Journeyman's Trade Model which we explored in *Managing*

Picasso is the transference of an understanding and appreciation of organizational culture.

Building Culture

Building a strong culture takes hard work and true commitment. An IT organization's leaders should put a set of boundaries around the organization to help shape its culture in a way that supports the organization from its mission to the outcomes it produces. While the culture building process is not something you can tick off in boxes, there are some fundamental building components to consider:

- **Dynamic and engaged leadership:** An outstanding culture is organic and evolving. It is fueled and inspired by leadership that possesses a real-time connection to the realities of the business. They genuinely care about the company's role in the larger world and are great communicators and motivators who set out a clearly communicated vision, mission, set of values, and goals and create an environment in which these can be realized. Leaders cannot single-handedly create culture, but without leadership's active involvement and support, the envisioned culture will not emerge and flourish.

- **Living values:** It is one thing to have basic beliefs and values framed and posted in the hallways—and these are actually quite common. But to truly impact culture, the organization must be guided by genuine and memorable values that employees see modeled throughout the organization daily. These values should be evident in the organization's people, products, working environment, and reflected in its internal and external communications. Most importantly, to achieve a values-driven culture, the organization must hire people using its values as a selection filter, and then motivate and measure its people against the way they model these values.

- **Accountability, freedom and responsibility:** One of the most important characteristics of a strong culture is that it will empower people, recognize their talents, make clear what they're accountable for, and give them the freedom and responsibility to deliver on those accountabilities. These are basic things, that when present will energize the best people to achieve truly great results, but many organizations fail to emphasize and nourish them sufficiently within their culture.

- **Celebrate success and learn from failure:** Companies that run at speed can sometimes forget to celebrate their accomplishments. In addition, fast-paced work can make it difficult for such organizations to take the time to acknowledge and learn from their failures. However, a strong culture will encourage both of these actions. Celebrating true success is motivating and energizing for people, and builds a sense of pride for the organization; recognizing failure and learning from it is the hallmark of a mature organizational culture and increases the organization's chances for future success.

As an abstraction, it is difficult to precisely define organizational culture, but it is not difficult to identify some of its most salient characteristics. For example:

- Culture takes time to create because of the nature of its two key ingredients: **trust** and **vision**
  - Trust requires a basis for its development provided by the IT organization's Guiding Principles
    - More specifically, these principles should address basic beliefs about things such as: technology, dealing with others, the organization's people, effective communication, effective leadership, effective management, and values

- The core belief system defined by such principles provides boundaries for decision-making that prove much more effective than a set of rigid, narrow rules or policies

  ○ Trust will grow as the organization matures providing that its leaders guide those in the evolving culture to have increased trust in the organization

  ○ Trust in the Guiding Principles can also provide a fly wheel effect to move the culture forward, provided that the organization demonstrates through its actions the application of these principles and how they support its success

  ○ Vision (to be discussed in more detail in Part III) formulates a picture of the future that achieves these two primary goals: (1) it should be crafted in a precise and succinct way so that it can be quickly understood by those in the organization; and 2) it should include a rationale that inspires those in the organization to want to help achieve this future

  ○ Properly conceived and articulated, vision can act as an engine that drives the development and evolution of culture

- A positive culture is a great enabler of organizational achievement, but it is important to remember that such culture can also be fragile

- Culture can be destroyed very quickly if the organization takes actions which destroy the trust employees have in its Guiding Principles or the belief they have in its vision

The Importance of Culture

If there's any doubt about the value of investing time in building culture, research has demonstrated that there are significant benefits that come from a vibrant and energizing culture. For example, such a culture helps an organization to attain the following critical intangible elements driving employee behavior:

- **Focus:** Aligns the entire organization's efforts towards achieving its vision, mission, and strategic goals

- **Motivation:** Builds employee enthusiasm, dedication, loyalty, and retention

- **Connection:** Encourages cooperation and synergies among the organization's various internal units

- **Cohesion:** Provides consistency and encourages coordination and control within the organization

- **Spirit:** Shapes employee attitudes toward work, allowing the organization to be more efficient, effective, and resilient

The positive impact of a vibrant culture goes beyond the organization's internal boundaries as well. Such a culture can help win and retain customers, promote the company's brand, entice top talent to join the organization, attract investors, and build goodwill within the larger business context in which the organization operates.

Recognizing the central importance of organizational culture, the Bertelsmann Foundation, in partnership with the consulting firm Booz Allen Hamilton, organized in 2003 the Carl Bertelsmann Prize to be awarded to a company that best demonstrated exemplary corporate culture and leadership. An international commission of experts was formed to research and develop a set of **critical success factors attributable to corporate culture and leadership** to use in judging the competition. [7] The group identified ten such critical success factors as follows:

1. Common goal orientation
2. Corporate social responsibility
3. Commonly held beliefs, values, and attitudes

4. Independent and transparent corporate governance

5. Participative leadership and management

6. Entrepreneurial behavior

7. Continuity of leadership

8. Ability to adapt, innovate, and integrate

9. Customer service orientation

10. Shareholder value orientation

Three Pillars of an IT Culture

The I/S Division of BlueCross BlueShield of South Carolina has identified three fundamental and inter-related concepts that we believe can serve as pillars for an IT organization's culture: Responsible Freedom, Humanity, and Justice:

- **Responsible Freedom**: Within the Hierarchical Matrix organizational structure, all people are given the **freedom** and **responsibility** within their assigned roles for getting the help they need from others to achieve the successful outcomes that they are accountable for.

- **Humanity**: Both Hierarchical and Matrix Leaders should inspire both great teamwork and outstanding individual effort by exemplifying the quality of **being helpful** to persons within their power or influence.

- **Justice**: Both Hierarchical and Matrix Leaders should support the moral principles resulting in **just conduct**.

Responsible Freedom

As we described in *Picasso on a Schedule,* IT work—especially software development—has long been recognized as a complex combination of art and science. Software developers utilize no tangible materials at all to create their desired products. Brooks [8] makes this point eloquently in his essay "*The Tar Pit*," in which he states that the programmer creates pure "thought stuff." In order to create pure "thought stuff" IT professionals, both programmers as well as the technical support staff that provide computing platforms on which the programs run, must have the *freedom* that creative work requires.

On the other hand, IT systems are always created for a specific purpose and use, and objective criteria will be applied to assess whether or not these systems live up to the expectations of their intended purpose. Hence the IT professional must work within the constraints of producing systems that satisfy the requirements that gave rise to their creation in the first place. In other words, IT professionals must be *responsible* for producing specific constrained outcomes.

The key to success in this enterprise is to *balance* the freedom necessary for the creativity needed with the responsibility necessary to constrain the outcomes to a specific set of requirements and a given timetable. The culture of an IT organization must help define a work environment which fully supports this balance. We believe the following principles, which provide IT professionals with the Responsible Freedom that enables them to deliver this balance, will help achieve such a culture.

- An IT organization should be committed to excellence. In all dealings with its clients or working internally with one another, everyone in the organization should be committed to excellence. Mediocrity and half-hearted efforts should not be tolerated, because anything less than a full commitment to excellence will erode the reputation the organization has worked so hard to build.

- Outstanding service is essential. In the end, any IT organization's product is service. This being so, the organization should recognizes the overriding importance of outstanding service to its clients and their customers. The organization's reputation will depend on how well it serves and satisfies its clients.

- IT employees should be expected to continually acquire and share knowledge to increase personal value and contribute to the organization. Knowledge sharing is a major form of contribution to the success of any IT organization.

- IT organizations that deliver technology solutions supporting a business, must understand that technology itself is never a primary cause of either greatness or decline in a business. Hence such an organization should avoid technology fads and bandwagons, recognizing that it cannot make good use of technology until it knows which technology is relevant to the business it supports.

- Technology can accelerate business momentum, but not create it. Therefore, in supporting a business, the wise IT organization will exercises the discipline to say "no" to the use of technology. The mantra "crawl, walk, run" should be such an organization's approach to technology change.

- An IT organization should strive to be organizations of "doers," recognizing that one of the greatest pleasures in life is doing what others say cannot be done.

- IT employees should "think like a challenger," doing their jobs with a sense of urgency and determination. They should always be attacking!

- The best systems are built by people who understand how the systems are actually used. In supporting a business, an IT organization should be completely focused on how it can make its clients' business easier, faster, and/or more efficient, whether their customer interaction is self-service or full-service.

- Good communication is never an accident. It is a deliberate act performed through planning. Those in an IT organization should be expected to take the time to effectively communicate and ensure vital information is shared.

- Choosing the right message and tone is vital to sending the right message. Too much detail at the wrong time confuses stakeholders. Not communicating also confuses stakeholders. The proper alignment of tone and intent minimizes confusion and results in more successful communication.

- Communication is a two-way street. Listening is a major part of communication. The receiver of a message must use effective techniques to understand the true intent of the communication.

- In the Hierarchical Matrix structure, the escalation process (introduced and discussed in Chapter 1) is your friend! The communications initiated by this process enable the Matrix to self-correct on the majority of issues that arise as it does the work of the organization. Within this structure, escalation should be used without hesitation when needed.

Humanity

Because IT is a creative endeavor, an IT organization's people— the source of its creativity—are its most valuable and essential resource. The effective IT organization will leverage this resource for optimal benefit to produce great client value. As we discussed in *Managing Picasso*, such leveraging is enhanced by a specialization strategy that provides people with the expertise necessary to produce excellent client solutions, as well as the productivity to make the organization efficient enough to deliver these solutions at reasonable cost, thereby supplying the value that clients demand.

However, the more specialized people are, the more interdependent they must become to produce the necessary overall organizational outcomes. Hence, the success of the organization will depend directly on creating a culture that supports an *energized community of specialized people working together*. Such a culture must support and recognize two fundamental but contradictory basic human impulses, namely that we love and need one another, yet we crave privacy and autonomy. Hence the successful culture must support the common humanity that binds people together and allows them to function as a group, but which also drives their need for individual accomplishment and self-actualization, recognizing that both these characteristics must be enabled to achieve common goals. We believe the following principles will help achieve such a culture.

- The individual employee is important. Both Hierarchical and Matrix Leaders should recognize the uniqueness of the individual. By treating people as individuals, you can release their full potential. Only then can you build a team of confident, creative people possessing a high degree of initiative and self-discipline. This results in the creation of a personally rewarding environment.

- Get and keep the right people. When hiring people, an IT organization should look beyond technical skills and place a greater weight on character attributes: work ethic, character, basic intelligence, dedication to fulfilling commitments, and ingrained values.

- To effectively support the use of technology within a business, the IT organization should employ people who can think like businesspeople, recognizing that this may require more development and training.

- Outstanding people must be identified within the organization and provided opportunity. The truly outstanding person seeks opportunities to grow personally and professionally, to contribute, to be challenged, to achieve, to be recognized, and to advance. This is accomplished by putting your best people on your biggest opportunities, and not always relegating them to your biggest problems.

- Competition for titles does not drive great behavior. The truly outstanding person competes against the job they are given, not other employees or for titles. A simple truth is that the right people at any level of the organization will do the right things and deliver the best results they are capable of, regardless of the incentive system.

- We believe that great teamwork occurs only when the following two behavioral principles are adhered to:

    ○ Leave the ego at the door. Work as a team playing off each member's strengths and watching out for each member's weaknesses.

    ○ Leave no fingerprints. Approach working with others in a modest and gracious manner. Act with quiet, calm determination to get the job done. Apportion credit for success to others, and accept apportioned responsibility when things go wrong.

Justice

As noted earlier, the Hierarchical Matrix is based on a specialization strategy centered on processes, which we believe provides the appropriate framework for nurturing people to grow and contribute to the organization's success. When a matrix structure is combined with specialization the organization can provide dynamic allocation of the specific expertise needed for each project's objectives. However, this structure presents some special challenges in managing the IT workforce.

For example, staff will typically be assigned to multiple projects simultaneously, and so prioritizing one's workload requires careful planning. And, because IT work is highly creative, and as a consequence unpredictable, such work planning itself a challenging task. Of course, IT work must be done within budgets and schedules, and so it is necessary to effectively structure and to manage the work to meet these constraints. And management's expectations about this work management should always be tempered by an awareness of the challenges inherent in creative work.

While these challenges can be daunting, we believe that IT professionals will overcome, and even welcome, these challenges given the right culture. The concepts of Responsible Freedom and Humanity that we just discussed are essential elements of such a culture. But there is a third concept that we believe binds the previous two concepts together into a successful culture, and that is the concept of Justice. The concept of Justice hinges on all people within an IT organization supporting the moral principles determining *just conduct*.

When everyone believes, and sees clear evidence, that the organization's behavior is driven by these moral principles, each person will have the confidence that they will be treated fairly and justly. Under these conditions, people are willing to make the necessary commitments and sacrifices to produce the excellent individual effort and effective teamwork required to surmount challenges and help the organization achieve greatness. We believe the following principles will help achieve a culture embodying Justice.

- Lines of communication must be kept open. Effective communication requires the flow of information up, down, and across the organization in order to communicate ideas, instructions, information, and feelings.

- The IT organization should practice an "open door" access to any level of management. Employees should feel free to ask to see any higher level of the management chain if they cannot resolve an issue within a given management level.

- All employees should strive for professionalism, always acting in a professional manner and respecting the rights and dignity of others. Anything less is unacceptable and should not be tolerated.

- The right balance between caring for employees' well-being and retaining objectivity to fairly evaluate employee performance must be maintained.

- Employees should be guided by the following behavioral principles:

  ○ Be direct. This is an attitude. Do not mince words; question everything.

- ○ No excuses. Quickly admit a problem, confront it, and never be defensive.

- ○ No victory laps. Celebrate for a nanosecond, determine what could have been done better, and then move on!

- It must be recognized that everyone makes mistakes, and that making mistakes is a sign of learning. But learning is not taking place if the same mistakes are made again and again, and when an employee is exhibiting patterns of mistakes, corrective action must be taken. This is necessary for the benefit of the employee in question as well as those on his or her team.

- The purpose of bureaucracy is to compensate for incompetence and lack of discipline within a small percentage of people. When a people change is necessary, management must be willing to act for the benefit of the overall organization!

- A simple way to evaluate proposed decisions is to answer the following questions:

  - ○ Is it right?

    - ▪ Is the decision morally right?

    - ▪ Is the decision technically right?

  - ○ Does it "make sense"?

    - ▪ Does the decision make "common sense"?

    - ▪ Does the decision make "dollars and cents"?

  - ○ If the answer to all the questions is "yes", you have a high probability of making a good decision.

Chapter 5

The Face of Culture

If you are lucky enough to be someone's employer, then you have a moral obligation to make sure people look forward to coming to work in the morning.

John Mackey
Whole Foods Market

As we have discussed, culture is an abstraction comprising a complex blend of human behavior, attitudes, assumptions, and beliefs. But this abstraction is expressed in various levels that make it easier for people to understand and embrace. These levels form the "face of the culture" for those who work in it, and provide a mechanism for organizations to nurture a commonly understood culture. Such understanding of culture in turn binds the organization together and can become a powerful flywheel that helps sustain its success.

The Levels of Culture

While every organizational culture will be different, we believe that there are five common levels at which culture is expressed:

- Symbols
  - Symbols are explicit and observable signs and artifacts that an employee is made aware of in their first few days working in an organization

- Environment
  - The environment comprises the general working conditions that characterize the organization

- Observable Behavior
  - The readily observed behavior that consists of norms, protocols, and informal rules that define the way work is accomplished in the organization

- Guiding Principles
  - Guiding principles are the espoused beliefs and inherent values that capture the ideals, goals, and aspirations of the organization and provide guidelines for the kind of behavior people in the organization are expected to embrace

- Underlying Assumptions
  - These assumptions, some conscious, some unconscious, may be expressed in shared basic beliefs and approaches, myths, stories, and oral histories that provide a strong sense of identity, belonging, and self-esteem to those in the organization

As illustrated in Figure 5.1, each level of culture depends on the levels below it. Underlying Assumptions form the deepest layer, with Guiding Principles based on these and making them more tangible. Observable Behavior should embody, and be consistent with, the Guiding Principles. The Guiding Principles, in turn, should be reflected in the Environment and the Symbols levels which are the two most immediately evident levels within the culture. Collectively, these layers define the Face of the Culture for an organization, and the effectiveness of the culture will be a function of the consistency and self-reinforcing nature of the relationships between these levels.

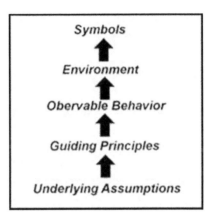

Figure 5.1: *The Relationships among the Five Levels of Culture*

The most central issues for leaders are to have a deep understanding of these various levels of culture, to continuously assess the rationale and functionality of assumptions made at each level, and to help the organization deal with the anxiety that is unleashed when those assumptions might be challenged during periods of organizational change.

To explore these different levels of culture more fully, we will describe some common ways they might be expressed and illustrate with a case study of specific examples of these expressions within the I/S Division of BlueCross BlueShield of South Carolina.

Culture Expressed in Symbols

As noted, cultural symbols are explicit and readily observable characteristics that all employees will be aware of. New employees will notice these and form their first impressions of organizational culture based on them within their first few days working in an organization. Common cultural symbols include the way work spaces are laid out and organized, the expectations for attire, common protocols for the way people greet each other with respect to titles and position, and physical access to facilities (like parking and security).

Here are specific examples taken from the I/S Division culture:

- **Offices and Work Space**
  - ○ Office configuration is standard for all levels of management
  - ○ All non-management employees are provided a standard configuration cube that is 6 x 7

- **Attire**
  - ○ The appropriate attire for the I/S Division is designated as "business casual"
  - ○ The IT Senior Staff often wears business attire, which may or may not include jackets and ties
  - ○ When external guests are on-site for meetings or consulting engagements, the management staff will dress appropriately for the audience they are entertaining

- **Titles and Prefixes**
  - ○ Formal salutations such as Mr., Ms., or Mrs. are not part of the I/S culture. Both management and non-management are addressed on a first name basis for most greetings and references.
  - ○ Situation with Outside Guests
    - ■ When formally introducing peers or organizational superiors at meetings with outside guests, it is tradition to state both the first and last name, and specify their role or title
  - ○ Situations with Internal Staff Only

- During meetings or social settings with internal staff, introductions are often self-initiated. For example, everyone introduces themselves around the room. In this case, most will state their name and where they work, titles are usually *not stated* unless they have some relevance to the meeting.

- *Parking*
  - Only the senior corporate officers of the company have a designated parking area
  - The remainder of the facility is designated as either open parking or management parking

- *Security*
  - All facilities are highly secured with normal access by an appropriate security badge
  - All visitors (non-employees) must be signed in and escorted by an employee who has access to the visitor's intended destination
  - Access to various computer systems is strictly controlled and employees are issued access appropriate to the duties they perform
  - Insofar as possible, new employees are given the appropriate system access so that they may begin their work as soon as possible after they arrive and have been oriented to the work environment

Culture Expressed in Environment

The environment comprises those elements of the culture that define working conditions. Common cultural environmental elements include the composition of the workforce, the way work is organized, the typical assignment of work to teams and individuals, the norms for working hours, and the organization's expectations and provisions for life-work balance.

To illustrate, here are some specific examples within the I/S Division culture:

- **The Workforce**
  - Traditionally, the I/S Division has been comprised of a senior and tenured staff. Most new management has typically been selected from within the organization. For instance, the CIO has been a member of the company for over 35 years, and the majority of his direct reports have been working with him for 20 years or more. This has provided a very stable management team whose members have years of experience working together, and who have successfully managed many ups and downs of the business environment.

  - But, the I/S staff has grown significantly over the past 15 years. In so doing, the demographics of the organization have changed considerably. Many managers and non-management employees have been newly introduced to the I/S organization's workforce, and bring with them a host of new ideas, new challenges, and diverse experiences to the organization. In addition to these new employees, the organization has utilized hundreds of new contractors that contribute to the workforce and help mold the organization's values, goals and culture.

  - While many new faces dot the landscape, there is still a healthy respect for the tenured employees that have significant knowledge about the organization highly integrated systems. New employees may sometimes find these tenured employees a bit resistant to change or quick to recite the standard lines of "it won't work here" or "that's been tried before and it didn't work." But these new employees should recognize that it is human nature for those who have been with the organization for a long time and been a part of its remarkable success to be resistant to change. Hence they should not be discouraged, but continue presenting ideas and suggestions, because there is in fact ample opportunity to blend their new ideas with their more senior colleagues' experience to advance the organization's success.

o The I/S Division is a very diverse organization, with many ethnic backgrounds and international cultures that have merged and blended with its traditional southern style. The diversity of the staff is one the organization's strengths and a significant factor in making it competitive in the market place.

o The I/S Division has enjoyed a very low turnover of valued staff over the past 15 years. The cost savings realized by not having to recruit, hire, and train new staff has allowed the organization to redirect its efforts to enhancing the professional skills of the loyal ongoing staff. In fact, the organization's commitment to providing a full range of professional development opportunities for staff has not only provided them with great personal growth but also made them key contributors to the organization's success.

- **Work Environment**

    o Susan Cain has noted that today's general business culture seems to hold that creativity and achievement come primarily from working in collaborative groups. Indeed most of us now work in teams, in offices without walls, in environments that seem to prize people skills above all. Culturally, we are often so impressed by charisma that we overlook the quiet part of the creative process. Lone geniuses are out. Collaboration is in. Virtually all American workers now spend time on teams and some 70 percent inhabit open-plan offices, in which no one has "a room of one's own." [9]

    o The I/S Division's culture recognizes that *some* teamwork is fine and offers a fun, stimulating, useful way to exchange ideas, manage information and build trust. However, the organization also recognizes that it is one thing to associate with a group in which each member works autonomously on his piece of the puzzle; it is another to be corralled into endless meetings or conference calls conducted in offices that afford no respite from the noise and gaze of co-workers. In fact, various studies show that open-plan offices can make workers hostile, insecure and distracted. They're also more likely to suffer from high blood pressure, stress, the flu and exhaustion. And people whose work is interrupted make 50% more mistakes and take twice as long to finish it.

○ People in groups often tend to sit back and let others do the work; they instinctively mimic others' opinions and lose sight of their own; and, often succumb to peer pressure. The Emory University neuroscientist Gregory Berns found that when we take a stance different from the group's, we activate the amygdala, a small organ in the brain associated with the fear of rejection. Berns calls this "the pain of independence." [10]

○ Much of the work performed in any IT organization is project-based and crosses many functional areas. Therefore, the work environment needs to provide a collaborative, consensus, and team-based atmosphere but at the same time allow for privacy and freedom from interruption. Solitude has long been associated with creativity and transcendence. As Picasso said, "Without great solitude, no serious work is possible." It is not surprising that most humans have two contradictory impulses: we love and need one another, yet we crave privacy and autonomy.

○ Because of the collaborative nature of IT projects, the I/S Division staff are comfortable discussing their work, their technical challenges or asking coworkers for their thoughts and recommendations whenever and wherever the discussion might ensue. It is not uncommon to hear passionate discussion in the elevators, hallways, conference areas or even the cafeteria. Everyone is engaged in helping to solve problems, finding solutions and taking the opportunity to pass on their tacit knowledge to their colleagues.

○ But decades of research show that individuals almost always perform better than groups in both quality and quantity, and group performance gets worse as group size increases. The organizational psychologist Adrian Furnham observed, "If you have talented and motivated people, they should be encouraged to work alone when creativity or efficiency is the highest priority." [11]

○ And research conducted by psychologists Mihaly Csikszentmihalyi and Gregory Feist seems to confirm this because it strongly suggests that high-achieving people are more creative when they enjoy privacy and freedom from interruption. They're extroverted enough to exchange and advance ideas, but see themselves as independent and individualistic. They're not joiners by nature. [12, 13]

○ Privacy also makes us more productive according to consultants Tom DeMarco and Timothy Lister who compared the work of more than 600 computer programmers at 92 companies. They found that people from the same companies performed at roughly the same level— but that there was a very significant performance gap between organizations. Surprisingly, the distinguishing factors were not related to greater experience or better pay, but rather how much privacy, personal workspace and freedom from interruption they enjoyed. Sixty-two percent of the best performers said their workspace was sufficiently private compared with only 19 percent of the worst performers! And 76% of the worst programmers said that they were often interrupted needlessly compared to only 38% of the best. [14]

○ Because much of IT work involves deep thinking and concentration, the I/S Division's technical areas are usually "do not disturb" zones. Staff is encouraged to take conversations to conference areas, lobbies or managers' offices, so that a serene and private atmosphere is maintained in the work areas.

- *Work Balance*

○ While the I/S work schedule is very demanding, and the challenges are nearly limitless, the organization encourages a strong sense of balance between working hard and having adequate time for one's personal life and family. Everyone is encouraged to take appropriate time off for vacations and regular breaks from the high pace and high stress of the 24 hours a day, 7 days a week world that we live in.

○ In addition to vacation breaks, much of the staff take full advantage of daily work breaks. These breaks serve as excellent networking opportunities and many times are extended into brainstorming sessions or opportunities for staff to discuss new technologies or particular challenges that they may be facing. A significant amount of knowledge sharing and ideas are exchanged during these quick, get-away breaks.

- *Hours Of Work*

○ As most of our staff are professionals and designated as exempt employees, it is understood the work hours are whatever it takes to get the job done.

○ Employees are authorized to negotiate flex time with their manager. Some employees work evenings or nights based on the duties assigned. Various alternate work schedules have been approved to accommodate these shift workers.

○ While a 40-hour work week is prescribed, most of our professional staff put in considerably more hours than that. Because of their chosen careers, most understand that additional hours per week are more the norm than the exception. A 45 to 50 hour week is not entirely unusual for most of the professional staff, who often work weekends, evenings, and other unscheduled times when performing on-call duties. Management has the authority to grant special absences for their employees when the overtime hours become excessive.

Culture Expressed in Observable Behavior

Observable behavior demonstrates the norms, protocols, and informal rules that define the way work is accomplished in the organization. There will be many examples of these behaviors, but all should be consistent with the expectations articulated in the organizational structure, the structure of project work, and organization's Guiding Principles (to be discussed next).

To illustrate, here are some specific examples within the I/S Division culture:

- *Titles versus Roles*
  - Many organizations have hierarchical, command-and-control structures where titles are extremely important. They clearly define the individual's position in the organization and their span of control. This is not the case in an IT organization using the Hierarchical Matrix organizational structure. Instead of titles which define a person's authority, responsibility, and span of control based on reporting structure within an organization, such an organization will use roles which define a person's authority, responsibility, and span of control relative to their work regardless of reporting structure.
  - The Hierarchical Matrix organizational structure does provide a traditional command-and-control structure. We call this part of the structure the Hierarchy, and its purpose is to manage all IT resources, with special focus

on the care and management of employees. Within the Hierarchy, the I/S Division has four recognized management roles. They are manager, director, assistant vice president, and vice president.

○ The Hierarchical Matrix IT organizational structure also provides a framework of highly developed repeatable processes based on a collaborative, consensus, and team-based atmosphere through which people come together for problem-solving and process management. We call this structure the Matrix. Within the Matrix, there are several "oversight roles" which are required based on the process framework for people to come together for problem-solving and process management, regardless of where they report within the Hierarchy.

○ Within a given highly developed repeatable process, these oversight roles are given managerial-like responsibilities and tasks that include the authority to make decisions and provide direction for work management. Without these roles, that responsibility would fall to the first level of management.

○ An example of such a recognized oversight role would be the role of project leader. A project leader is primarily responsible for the successful completion of a given project. Project team members, in the Matrix, take direction concerning the project from the project leader. This direction includes but is not limited to things like task completion dates, overtime, and time off. Other examples of recognized oversight roles include work scheduler and estimate coordinator.

- *Healthy Dissent*

  ○ While it is true that the I/S organization works in a team-based and collaborative environment, there is a fair amount of friendly conflict and healthy dissent in many meetings and work sessions. A variety of opinions are both welcomed and encouraged, and individuals' passion for their work is often evident in the discussions.

○ Everyone is encouraged to think and to contribute ideas and experiences to the discussions. Brainstorming is a common method of problem solving. Everyone has a voice and everyone is encouraged to put their two cents into the debate.

- *Pay For Performance – Contributions Matter*

○ The I/S organization does NOT reward tenure, nor base compensation on tenure. Employees are paid for the depth and breadth of knowledge they are able to demonstrate through the successful accomplishment of their assignments, and the value that they contribute to the success of the organization.

- *Networking*

○ The ability to network and to establish working relationships with individuals in all areas of the I/S organization is absolutely essential to a person's success within the organization. Things get done through people!

○ Anyone new to the I/S organization should spend a significant part of his or her first six months learning who is who and understanding the basic way the workforce is organized.

○ Gaining an understanding of the various lines of business, who supports what functions, what their responsibilities are, and where they are located is essential.

○ Networking is about relationships. The more successful a person is at building relationships, the quicker he or she will feel like an effective contributing member of the organization.

- *Heroes*

○ Every organization has its heroes. The stories of the organization's heroes can make up the very fabric of its culture. Everyone loves a great story about how the hero, armed with knowledge and experience, arrives just in time to get the project back on track, to solve the technical problem, or to provide the answer.

o Having heroes or 'experts' who are acknowledged to be the 'go to' people within an organization is necessary for the overall success of that organization. These experts' successes are championed, their contributions rewarded, and their 'heroism' applauded.

o But building an organization's culture based solely on having heroes does not work in the long run, especially as an IT enterprise grows in size, complexity, and diversity. In fact, a culture based on heroes will turn the heroes into prima donnas which will ultimately be destructive to the organization.

o The I/S organization recognizes that knowledge sharing is the key to sustaining its successful culture. Knowledge sharing requires the valued staff members, the 'heroes', to pass on their tacit knowledge to the generations coming after them to meet the organization's need to expand its cadre of experts in the future. Hence the 'heroes' success cannot be defined by the number of times they are the answer. We need our 'heroes' to become the *teachers* of our future experts!

Culture Expressed in Guiding Principles

Guiding Principles are the espoused beliefs that provide boundaries for the kind of behavior people in the organization are expected to exhibit. It is important to note that these principles are not intended as hard and fast rules, but as guidelines that require good judgment and tacit knowledge about the organization and human nature to be applied effectively.

The I/S organization has over time developed a set of more than 40 Guiding Principles, organized within five major categories: Technology, Dealing with Others, Our People, Effective Communication, and Effective Management. Note that a number of these Guiding Principles are embedded in the Three Pillars of Culture that we discussed in the previous chapter. The complete set is given here:

- *Technology*

  - <u>Technology itself is never a primary cause of either greatness or decline in a business</u>. Avoid technology fads and bandwagons. Recognize that you cannot make good use of technology until you know which technology is relevant to the business it supports. Technology can accelerate business momentum, but not create it. Therefore, you need the discipline to say no to the use of technology. Crawl, walk, run is a very effective approach to technology change!

  - <u>Beware those who fear being "left behind"</u>! Those who build and perpetuate mediocrity are motivated by the fear of being left behind, especially as it pertains to technology.

  - <u>We are "doers"</u>. The greatest pleasure in life is doing what others say cannot be done.

  - <u>Keep your eye on the goal</u>. Inventing the "Next Big Thing" is not the goal. Building the "Current Big Thing" better than anyone else *is* the goal. We are not Alpha inventors, we are Beta improvers!

  - <u>The Goal: 100% Self-Service</u>. Everyone in I/S is completely focused on how they can make our client's business easier, faster, and/or more efficient, whether the customer interaction is self-service or full-service.

  - <u>The best systems are built by people who understand how the systems are actually used</u>. Because we tend to develop our own code, we look for people who can think like businesspeople, which requires a lot more development and training.

- ○ <u>Build-it-once-for-all mentality</u>. When we write code, we automate, enhance, and change processes, incorporating logic to meet a current business need into our core systems. This provides a base to build on to meet future business needs.

- ○ <u>Do-it-yourself approach to Core Application Development</u>. We tend to manage Core Application Systems Development from programming to process engineering, which means there is no peer group support or industry best-practice knowledge from others using the same application. Therefore, we must double our efforts to find independent verification that what we develop provides a competitive operational platform for our client's business.

- • *Dealing with Others*

  - ○ <u>Outstanding service is essential</u>. Our product *is* service. This being so, we must recognize the overriding importance of outstanding service to the customer. Our reputation depends on how well we serve and satisfy today's clients.

  - ○ <u>We are committed to excellence</u>. In all dealings with our clients or working internally with one another, we are committed to excellence. Mediocrity and half-hearted efforts have no place in I/S. Anything less than a full commitment to excellence will erode the reputation we have worked so hard to build.

  - ○ <u>Leave the ego at the door</u>. Work as a team playing off each member's strengths and watching out for each member's weaknesses.

  - ○ <u>Leave no fingerprints</u>. Approach working with others in a modest and gracious manner. Act with quiet, calm determination to get the job done. Apportion credit for success to others, and accept apportioned responsibility when things go wrong.

- ○ <u>Be direct</u>. This is an attitude. Do not mince words; question everything.

- ○ <u>No excuses</u>. Quickly admit a problem, confront it, and never be defensive.

- ○ <u>Think of us as a challenger</u>. Do your job with a sense of urgency and determination. Always be attacking!

- ○ <u>No victory laps</u>. Celebrate for a nanosecond, determine what could have been done better, and then move on!

- *Our People*

  - ○ <u>When hiring, get the right people</u>. Place a greater weight on character attributes: work ethic, character, basic intelligence, dedication to fulfilling commitments, and ingrained values. When in doubt, don't hire – keep looking.

  - ○ <u>The individual employee is important</u>. I/S managers should recognize the uniqueness of the individual. By treating people as individuals, we can release their full potential. Only then can we build a team of confident, creative people possessing a high degree of initiative and self-discipline. This results in the creation of a personally rewarding environment.

  - ○ <u>Opportunity must be provided</u>. The truly outstanding person seeks opportunities to grow personally and professionally, to contribute, to be challenged, to achieve, to be recognized, and to advance. I/S managers must identify outstanding people and work to provide them opportunity. Put your best people on your biggest opportunities, not your biggest problems.

  - ○ <u>Competition for titles does not drive our behavior</u>. The truly outstanding person competes against the job they are given, not other employees or for titles. Compete to grow personally and professionally, to contribute, to be challenged, to achieve, to be recognized, and to advance.

- ○ <u>Knowledge Sharing is a major form of contribution</u>. Employees are expected to continually acquire and share knowledge with other employees to increase personal value and contribute to the organization.

- ○ <u>Rewards are based on contribution</u>. Simple truth: The right people at any level of the organization will do the right things and deliver the best results they are capable of, regardless of the incentive system. Those employees who are best able to take advantage of the opportunities provided will receive the greatest compensation.

- ○ <u>Understand and practice the concept of "professional distance"</u>. I/S managers must maintain the right balance between caring for employees' well-being and retaining objectivity to fairly evaluate employee performance.

- ○ <u>Making mistakes is a sign of learning</u>. Everyone makes mistakes. It is a sign of learning as long as the same mistakes are not made again and again. Deciding when an employee is exhibiting patterns of mistakes is sometimes tough, but it must be done and corrective action must be taken.

- ○ <u>Get rid of the few and lessen the need for bureaucracy!</u> The purpose of bureaucracy is to compensate for incompetence and lack of discipline within a small percentage of people. When you need to make a people change, act!

- • *Effective Communication*

  - ○ <u>Good communication is never an accident</u>. It is the deliberate act performed through planning. Take the time to effectively communicate and ensure vital information is shared.

  - ○ <u>Communications is the glue that binds decision-making and processes</u>. Decision-making relies on effective delivery of specific messages designed around six components:

- What—Key points to convey to stakeholder or group.

- Why—A rationale for engaging them (from big picture to detailed action).

- Who—A list of recipients to engage.

- When—The timing and frequency of communications.

- How—The method of delivery (face-to-face, newsletter, phone, e-mail, etc.).

- What's Next—The feedback loop: a mechanism to collect feedback, when appropriate.

o Choosing the right message and tone is vital to sending the right message. Too much detail at the wrong time confuses stakeholders. Not communicating also confuses stakeholders. The proper alignment of tone and intent minimizes confusion and results in more successful communication.

o Communication is a two-way street. Listening is a major part of communication. The receiver of the message must use effective techniques just like the sender.

o The Escalation Process is your friend! Our Escalation Process enables the Matrix with the ability to self-correct on the majority of issues that arise as it does the work of IT. When the Escalation Process does result in reaching out to the Hierarchy for help, you should receive the escalation with a positive attitude: "Thank you for bringing this to my attention, so how can I help with the issue?" You must remember the Escalation Process does not recognize a formal organizational communication path; it only contains guidance concerning the nature of what a "proper escalation" should be. In the end, an escalation should be viewed as a cry for help and your primary concern at this point is to help get the work done!

- *Effective Management*

  ○ <u>Be results oriented</u>. This is our first operating principle. Over the long term, end results will indicate our success.

  ○ <u>I/S managers are first and foremost technologists</u>. In the May 20, 2002 edition of USA Today, the lead article's headline read, "Companies squander billions on tech." The article continued, "In the go-go days of the 1990s, firms spent wildly on software they really didn't need." In that same edition, the USA Today Snapshots headline was, "Technology not that important for CIO's – Only 10% of chief information officers say that technology proficiency is an important skill to be successful." The lack of proficiency in technology is why the lead headline had to be written! Our very reason for existing is the understanding of technology for the most cost-effective and efficient exploitation of that technology within the business of our clients.

  ○ <u>Pay attention to detail</u>. While some organizations manage by exception, we believe this will not work in I/S. Details are necessary in order to make good decisions. As a manager, you must have these details first-hand. You cannot operate effectively with limited or second-hand information. You need facts. So how much detail is enough? As a manager, you need to know enough detailed facts to ask the right questions to help your team and to know when you hear the right answers.

  ○ <u>Develop and retain outstanding people</u>. If we firmly believe that people are our most important resource, then we must build a team of truly outstanding people. Attracting, developing, and retaining these individuals is the responsibility of every manager, not only those needing more people.

  ○ <u>Get the job done</u>. Managing is not a job for the faint-hearted. You will face many demanding and difficult tasks. It is up to you to utilize all the resources at your disposal to get the job done. One of your most difficult tasks will be to maintain an effective balance between control and creative solutions to problems. We must never let our control mechanisms stand in the way of delivering outstanding service to our customers.

- <u>Keep the lines of communication open</u>. Effective communication requires the flow of information up, down, and across the organization. We communicate ideas, instructions, information, and feelings. As a manager, you bear the burden for initiating and encouraging this flow.

- <u>Practice an open door policy</u>. We actively practice the idea of "open door" access to any level of management. Employees may ask to see any higher level of the management chain if they cannot resolve an issue with a given management level. Normally, the management chain is followed, but our policy allows for the employee to approach any level of management without disclosing the subject to the intermediate levels of management.

- <u>Strive for professionalism</u>. As a manager, you are responsible for developing and providing the customer with outstanding professionals who consistently maintain professional attitudes. Encourage all employees to act in a professional manner and to respect the rights and dignity of others. Anything less is unacceptable and not to be tolerated. You must be capable of leading by example.

- <u>Planning (budgeting) is priceless, but Plans (budgets) are useless</u>. It is the process done right that provides value.

- <u>We operate best with scarce resources</u>. Having deadlines to work against limits the opportunity to waste our resources.

- <u>Worry about saving money, not saving face</u>. Reach for the heights of perfection while burrowing down into every last data point to save money.

- ○ <u>All costs are variable</u>. To operate a cost effective organization, we must take the view that all costs are variable over a particular time horizon and be willing to cut that cost.

- ○ <u>If you start with a blank sheet of paper, you're dead</u>. "Thinking outside the box" has come to mean thinking of a solution that is somehow outside of what you already know and do, and coming up with something wholly new. Pushing people to think outside the box doesn't work. Instead, our approach to innovation is to take an idea or solution that has been used somewhere else, combine a number of existing ideas or solutions, and introduce them as a solution never seen before.

- ○ <u>Maintain an attitude of healthy discontent</u>. Sound management requires a probing, inquiring mind. Satisfaction with the status quo should be avoided. As you carry out your responsibilities as a manager, intelligently question existing practices and procedures. Ensure the most effective, up-to-date methods are being used. Actions based on the rationale, "that's the way we've always done it" should be examined closely. As a manager, you must not be afraid to challenge precedent. Be alert for antiquated or improper practices, which must be changed.

- ○ <u>Exert authority when necessary</u>! Consensus decisions are often at odds with intelligent decisions. Sometimes you just have to make the decision and move on!

Culture Expressed in Underlying Assumptions

At the deepest level of culture are the underlying assumptions that are rooted in the core beliefs, formative experiences—both good and bad— and the most fundamental approaches that have helped the organization achieve its success over time. Some of these concepts will be conscious and made explicit, but others have become such a part of the "fabric of the organization" that they are in essence second nature to the organization's leaders and others who have been in the organization for substantial periods of time. The more subtle assumptions may be embedded in myths, stories, and oral histories of the organization. Together, these underlying assumptions are the basis for all the other levels of culture that we have discussed and are in large part what provides a shared sense of identity, belonging, pride, and self-esteem to those in the organization.

To illustrate, here are some specific examples of underlying assumptions within the I/S Division culture:

- Respect and Value People

  o This assumption forms the basis for the Three Pillars of Culture (discussed in some detail in Chapter 4) with their emphasis on Responsible Freedom, Humanity, and Justice—concepts which encompass and lead to many of the Guiding Principles we listed above

- Embrace Diversity in Getting the Best People for the Job

  o The organization's hiring practices focus on finding and acquiring the very best people available, without regard to age, gender, ethnicity, or religion, and the resulting diversity is one the organization's strengths

- Use an Evolutionary, Not Revolutionary, Approach

  o The I/S organization has taken a unique, evolutionary, and systematic approach in the development and implementation of its administrative and operational practices over the past 30 years, and that approach has enabled it to integrate IT staff as required while ensuring management philosophies and administrative and operational practices remain intact

- View IT as a "Business within a Business"

  o The I/S organization is run as a business by employing common best business practices that any successful non-IT business operates under, and by ensuring that all I/S managers possess both technical competency *and* business competency

- Employ Business-Driven Innovation

  ○ Such an approach means assessing opportunities for innovation from the client's perspective

- Adopt Systems Thinking

  ○ The I/S organization does this by employing the IT-OSD Model, discussed in depth in *Picasso on a Schedule* and reviewed in Chapter 2 of this book, as an overall decision-making framework

- Work with Modesty and Resolute Determination to Get the Job Done

  ○ The I/S organization believes that its ultimate success depends on being an organization of "doers" while at the same time maintaining a productive collaborative environment, both internally and with its clients, by approaching its work in a modest manner

- Be a Learning Organization

  ○ The I/S organization expects all staff to engage in continuous lifelong learning, and it provides opportunities for this through a range of educational programs that synthesize individual learning and organizational transformation

- Operate with the Highest Standards of Ethics and Integrity

  ○ One of the most valuable assets the I/S organization has is its reputation which is built on the excellence of its work *and* the confidence that its clients have in its integrity and adherence to high ethical standards

Part III
Vision and Leadership

Chapter 6

Create a Compelling Vision

*To the person who does not know where he wants to go there is
no favorable wind.*

Seneca

One of a leader's most central responsibilities is to lead and energize adaptive change. To do this effectively, a leader must attract followers and inspire them to pursue shared goals whose attainment will propel the organization to achieve long-term success as it moves into the future. A vital element within this process is the leader's ability to articulate and communicate a compelling vision.

What is Vision?

Vision, like culture, is largely an intangible entity, but when a leader is able to inspire followers through his or her vision for the organization's future, it can serve as a powerful engine driving the organization toward tangible excellence and sustainable success. Following Kotter [3], we define vision as follows:

A vision is a picture of the future with some implicit or explicit commentary, which can be described in five minutes or less and elicit a reaction that signifies both understanding and excitement, on why people should strive to create that future.

There are of course many definitions of vision, and there often exists confusion of the term vision with related terms such as *mission, strategy, organizational goals,* and *philosophy.* All of these terms describe important elements of an organization's overall culture and identity. A mission statement is about what an organization *is* and what it *intends to do.* Current strategy embodies the *logic* for how a mission can be achieved, and organizational goals are the *concrete measurable results* that verify that the strategy is successful. Finally, a philosophy is a description and rationale for the organization's *principles* and *values,* and as we have seen these principles and values serve as a foundation for the organization's culture. Indeed, the organization's *principles* and *values* are the unchanging bedrock upon which all of these other concepts are built.

In contrast, a vision points the direction toward an *ideal future* for the organization that its leader wants to create. Vision requires the leader of an organization to communicate the direction of the organization in words and deeds to all whose cooperation may be needed to achieve the vision. The mission, current strategy, and organizational goals are about today; an effective and compelling vision provides a *bridge* to get the organization to tomorrow. Leaders are responsible for motivating, inspiring, and energizing people, despite any obstacles, to accomplish an organization's vision by transforming and adapting its mission, strategy and organizational goals.

Elements of a Compelling Vision

Articulating a compelling vision requires *deep holistic thought.* Researchers have demonstrated that a useful model of the human brain focuses on how the two spatial hemispheres of the brain, referred to the "right brain" and the "left brain", offer different and complementary brain functions. In this model, the left brain is described as the part of the brain that addresses issues and problems in a more logical, analytical, and objective way, while the right brain tends to act in a more intuitive, subjective, holistic or "big picture" manner. Figure 6.1 illustrates this complementary nature of the right and left brains.

Both the right and left brains must be fully engaged and expertly blended to produce an authentic vison that will capture the hearts and minds of those in the organization and propel them to accomplish the vision against the inevitable obstacles. The ability to successfully apply such a thought process is not common and is beyond full description. But because the process is so important, we are providing the following description on how we believe this process works at a high level, based on the most recent research into this subject as of the writing of this book.

Clearly the complementary functions of the right and left brains must be integrated for the brain to perform its overall functions effectively, and hence communication across the right brain/left brain "barrier" is essential. The medial prefrontal cortex may be the specific part of the Human Brain (often referred to as *the interpreter*) that unifies the signals from the two halves to create a smooth, coherent decision that makes sense in a holistic way to the individual. This integration and unification of sometimes conflicting information is somewhat analogous to the process a CEO applies to arrive at conclusions and decisions in a business organization, sorting through ambiguity and uncertainty to establish order and direction.

A good example of how the two hemispheres both specialize *and* cooperate can be seen in the way we hear and comprehend speech. The left brain specializes in picking out the sounds or phonemes that form words and then working out the actual syntax of the words. On the other hand, the right brain is more sensitive to the emotional features of language, tuning in to the rhythms and cadence of speech that carry intonation and stress. Hence, it takes both sides of the brain to collect the appropriate information, and then the interpreter to synthesize and form a coherence using the input from both hemispheres to give us the incredible richness of our ability to hear and attach meaning to spoken language.

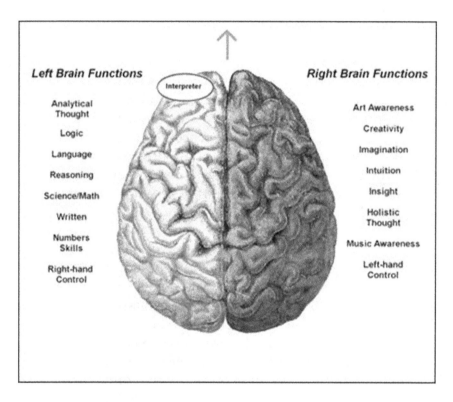

Figure 6.1: *A Model of the Human Brain*

In his book *The Future of the Mind* [15], the physicist Micho Kaku, while admitting that the human mind remains one of the greatest and most mysterious forces in the world, nonetheless probes the evolution of the human brain and proposes a Theory of the Mind and a Theory of Consciousness that attempt to describe some of the essential elements of human behavior. In particular, the two theories provide some interesting insight into our ability to create a vision of the future. The two relatively independent hemispheres of the human brain complement each other in this process by offering competing pessimistic versus optimistic and analytical versus holistic analyses of the same idea allowing the interpreter portion of our brain to engage in a type of internal thought debate.

In his Theory of the Mind, Kaku proposes that the firing of certain neurons are essential for mimicry and empathy which in turn give humans the ability not only to copy complex tasks performed by others but also to emulate the experience of emotions that another person must be feeling. This process allows humans to form alliances with others, isolate enemies, and solidify friendships, which in a complex society are the foundation for the ability to correctly guess the intentions, motives, and plans of other people. Such a capability clearly provides a tremendous survival advantage over those species which do not possess it.

Further, Kaku offers a definition and taxonomy of consciousness that includes the animal kingdom in which he defines consciousness as a function of how an organism utilizes feedback loops to modify its behavior. In the resulting spectrum of consciousness, creating a vision for the future appears to be a uniquely human capability. In his Space-Time Theory of Consciousness, he proposes a model of the world in which humans appear to be using multiple feedback loops in various views of the world (e.g. space, time, and our positions in relation to others) to evaluate the past and form simulations of the future that enable us to accomplish a goal. A simple example of this is the way children run simulations of the extremely sophisticated adult society by playing games such as doctor, cops and robbers, and school which allows a child to experiment with and analyze a small segment of adult behavior and then run his or her own simulations into the future. This ability to run simulations into the future forms the basis for the human ability to create visions for the future.

More specifically, we believe the Vision Quality of a given leader is dependent on his or her ability to perform this process of running simulations into the future described within the Space-Time Theory of Consciousness, while at the same time incorporating the process that allows humans to form alliances, isolate enemies and solidify friendships as described within the Theory of the Mind. While all humans have the ability to run simulations into the future, the quality and usefulness of the simulations can vary greatly from individual to individual. To put it more simply, there is a large qualitative difference along the future simulation spectrum between daydreams and visions for the future that might be applied to modify behavior in constructive ways to achieve future goals and objectives.

For a leader to form useful and applicable simulations into the future and create a compelling vision for his or her organization, these simulations and the resulting vision should be grounded in three essential elements:

- **Experience.** To create a compelling vision for an organization, a leader must have successful leadership experience, including:
  - Balancing change and continuity
  - Inspiring others to follow
  - Leading change
- **Deep Knowledge.** For a leader's vision to be realistic for the organization to implement, the leader must have deep knowledge of the organization itself, including:
  - The organization's fundamental capabilities
  - The organization's capacity to learn and adapt
  - The organization's culture
- **Earned Trust.** To engage followers and gain their commitment to implement a vision, a leader must have already earned followers' trust, which derives from a successful combination of the previous two components—experience and deep knowledge—that followers recognize and respect.

Figure 6.2 illustrates this overall process. Note that the input implicit in the experience, knowledge, and the trust that others have for the leader will contain a wide spectrum of information. Some of this information will be ambiguous, intuitive and very subjective, while other parts of it may be precise, analytical, and even quantitative. Additionally and even more importantly, there will be conflicting information within these categories, as well as between the categories. And, of course, there will always be information that the leader would wish to have that is unknown or perhaps even unknowable at the current moment in time.

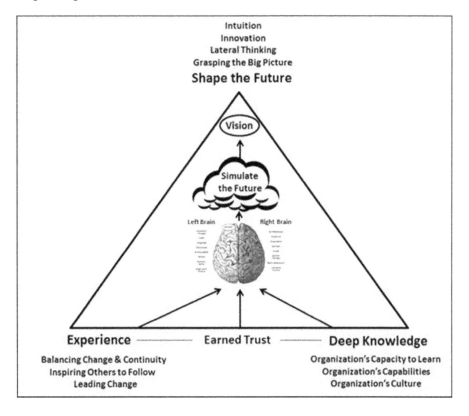

Figure 6.2: *The Human Brain and the Vision Quality of a Leader*

In summary, before the brain can even attempt the formulation of a coherent simulation of the future and its related vision, it must first sort through, filter, evaluate, apply value judgments to, and finally condense and abstract all the available input information much of which already resides in the brain itself. This is the essence of the complex *internal thought debate* we mentioned earlier that the interpreter portion of the brain facilitates between the left and right brain functions.

This is a daunting task and the wise leader will seek help in making sense of this potentially bewildering array of information and its many possible interpretations. Hence, a great leader will seek counsel from trusted people who can perform these processes well and communicate their thoughts and insights honestly and effectively. The leader must then work to be open-minded in listening to and considering many interpretations and proposed logical extensions, some of which he or she may not have previously concisely formulated or even thought about. But, in the end, the effective leader must accept the responsibility, and have the ability needed, to assimilate and articulate the information into a coherent meaningful vision of the future. And while a vision may benefit if it arrives from a consensus among a leadership team, it is absolutely essential that the leader believe deeply in the vision—whether or not it achieves a consensus.

Indeed, a major part of the leader's job once he or she has formulated a deeply held vision is to communicate that vision effectively and passionately to not only the organization's leadership team, but to the rank and file as well. A compelling vision is a vison rooted in the reality of the current organization's capabilities and culture, but which sets the direction for the organization's future success and inspires the people within the organization to internalize the vision so that it energizes the entire organization to move toward this future.

Vision and Strategy Revisited

As we noted earlier, vision and strategy are related but also fundamentally different. A compelling vision sets the organization's direction and inspires people to strive to achieve it. Strategy draws the actual roadmap about how the organization can get there. A well-thought out strategy which is not informed by a compelling vision may produce acceptable results, but will fail to achieve greatness. Likewise, a compelling vision without an accompanying effective strategy to implement it will produce frustration and lamentations about missed opportunities. Both a compelling vision and an effective strategy are required.

Great leaders will recognize the need for both vision and strategy, and will clearly understand that they are not one and the same. Because these are different, the leader must also realize that the abilities to produce them are not the same either. In other words, the person who formulates and passionately conveys the vision may not be person who can always find the best path for the organization to get to the envisioned future state.

Of course, the leader must have some concepts about enabling strategy as the vision is formed, otherwise the vision may be unrealistic and essentially unobtainable. This is why the grounding of a vision in experience and deep knowledge about the organization is so important. But the leader must guard against believing that he or she automatically has the best strategy forward. Certainly the leader must believe that such a strategy is achievable and within the strengths and capacity that he or she has envisioned for the organization. But working out the particular strategy that will achieve success requires deep thought on its own, and requires different thought processes than those involved in formulating the vision in the first place.

As we have pointed out previously, the ability to successfully apply such a thought process is not common. And while we have tried to describe how we believe this process works at a high level, the ability to apply this process with success is quite exceptional. The fact that visionary leaders are much studied, analyzed, and admired is evidence of their very rarity.

Formulating the strategy to accomplish or implement a vision requires a different kind of thought process, no less demanding, but with a different set of objectives and guiding parameters. In short, the process of formulating an effective strategy has the advantage of being *bounded* by the driving vision. In other words, the vision is there to guide the strategy and serve as the ultimate measure against which potential strategies can be evaluated, tested and, when necessary, refined. Once again, both the right and left brains will be engaged, but the left brain functions will drive the process. The objective here is find something that *works in practice*, hence analytical, logical thought will be at a premium, even though this must be tempered by intuition, passion, instinct, and consideration for its impact on the people who will implement the strategy. Great leaders will surround themselves with excellent people who are skilled at this process—developing, evaluating, refining, and ultimately implementing a strategy that effectively moves the organization toward an established and passionately held vision.

While some visionary leaders may also be the best strategists, this is not necessarily the case. Several examples from history will illustrate. One of the great visionary leaders of the 20th century—perhaps ever—was Sir Winston Churchill. Churchill became Prime Minister during one of the darkest periods in all of Britain's history. Following the German invasion of France and the subsequent over-running of French defenses in May, 1940, Neville Chamberlain resigned and Churchill became Prime Minister. His steadfast refusal to consider defeat, surrender, or a compromise peace inspired the British people's spirit of resistance at a time when a German invasion seemed imminent as Britain stood alone against Adolf Hitler and Nazi Germany (the US would not enter the war for another 18 months).

In a series of stirring speeches to Parliament in those early days, Churchill laid out the vision that helped sustain the British nation during these dark times. Indeed, excerpts from two of his early speeches still evoke a strong emotional response and echo powerfully 75 years later:

Even though large tracts of Europe and many old and famous States have fallen or may fall into the grip of the Gestapo and all the odious apparatus of Nazi rule, we shall not flag or fail. We shall go on to the end. We shall fight in France, we shall fight on the seas and oceans, we shall fight with growing confidence and growing strength in the air, we shall defend our island, whatever the cost may be. We shall fight on the beaches, we shall fight on the landing grounds, we shall fight in the fields and in the streets, we shall fight in the hills; we shall never surrender. (June 4, 1940) [16]

Two weeks later, Churchill returned to Parliament to exhort the nation to rise to the call of duty and hardship in accomplishing what must have seemed to most people the almost impossible task of prevailing against the Nazi juggernaut:

But if we fail, then the whole world, including the United States, including all that we have known and cared for, will sink into the abyss of a new dark age made more sinister, and perhaps more protracted, by the lights of perverted science. Let us therefore brace ourselves to our duty, and so bear ourselves that, if the British Empire and its Commonwealth lasts for a thousand years, men will still say, 'This was their finest hour.' (June 18, 1940) [17]

While Churchill was singularly inspirational in imparting his vison that unwavering devotion to duty and unyielding refusal to consider defeat would lead to ultimate victory, neither he nor anyone else in the British government or military had, in the spring of 1940, a comprehensive strategy to save Britain from a disastrous defeat. Even so, Churchill viewed himself as an expert strategist and promptly set out devising strategies that he believed would reverse Britain's fortunes. However his closest advisors, especially Sir Alan Brooke, Chairman of the Chiefs of Staff Committee, the foremost military advisor to Churchill throughout the war, and a far more skilled strategist, resisted many of Churchill's daring, but often ill-conceived, strategic initiatives.

In this resistance, Brooke displayed great courage, because Churchill was not an easy man to resist. He had the strength of personality and persistence in pushing for his own ideas that many found impossible to resist. However, to his credit and as a testament to the greatness of his leadership, Churchill did not run roughshod over strong advisors like Brooke, and eventually allowed others who were superior strategists to figure out how to achieve his vision. Without his willingness to allow Brooke and his other military advisors, and later US Generals George Marshall and Dwight Eisenhower, to formulate and carry out an effective strategy, victory over Nazi Germany may well not have been achieved.

A second example is provided by President Ronald Reagan. Reagan articulated and continuously reinforced his vision of the ultimate Cold War defeat of the Soviet Union—borrowing the phrase "Evil Empire" from the popular *Star Wars* movie series of the time as an energizing code phrase for his vision. He used this vision to inspire the American people to endure economic uncertainties and focus on the longer range goal of a world with reduced tensions and fewer prospects of nuclear devastation. Similar to Churchill, he appealed to patriotism and national pride in conveying and articulating this vision, grounded in the nation's basic values and history of sacrifice for greater causes.

Reagan, like Churchill, also left the specific strategies to be developed by trusted advisors and staff. Unlike Churchill, Reagan did not seem to view himself as the ultimate strategist and so he embraced more readily the strategic advice of his staff, led by the expert strategist Secretary of State Jim Baker, to articulate and refine the resulting strategies to accomplish the vision.

As a final example, the case of another visionary leader, Abraham Lincoln, demonstrates how his driving vision of preserving the Union, was nearly lost for lack of an effective war strategy. Though Lincoln realized that the strategies employed were ineffective, he did not take it on himself to devise the specific strategy needed, instead having the correct instinct to continue searching for the right strategic advisors and generals who could provide the winning strategy.

The point of all these examples is to reinforce the concept that vision and strategy, while intimately related, are in fact different in essential ways. The message for leaders is that creating and articulating a compelling vision is the responsibility of the leader, though input from others is essential and should be welcomed. However, the wise leader will realize that formulating a winning strategy for the vision requires a different thought process, and hence he or she must be open to guidance, advice, and even relinquishing the leading role, in the formulation and implementation of strategy. This is not however, to diminish the importance of the guiding and energizing vision in finding the right strategy, and in the next chapter, we will explore how this vision can accomplish this and also act as the primary enabler for the success of that strategy once it is devised.

Part IV
Transformative Change and Leadership

Chapter 7

Change, Vision, and Culture

There is nothing more difficult to take in hand, more perilous to conduct, or more uncertain in its success, than to take the lead in the introduction of a new order of things.

Niccolo Machiavelli

In today's rapidly changing business climate, it is unarguable that the ability to make adaptive change is a necessary survival skill. But the realization that change is necessary and the identification of the right kind of change and how it can be effectively implemented are two very different propositions. Successful organizations must become adept at both these challenges—recognizing the need for change *and* figuring out how to implement the needed changes effectively. In considering ways to meet these challenges, it is instructive to recognize that adaptive change can take two distinct forms—incremental change and transformative change.

Incremental change is much less daunting, though it still requires great skill and leadership in determining when and why change is needed, and then devising the right way to undertake the necessary change. Such change will often be monitored and even controlled by internal organizational governance processes. While such processes offer no guarantee of success, they can significantly reduce risk, help allay fears and uncertainties, and provide for controlled introduction and refinement of change, provided these processes have been carefully designed and refined over time. Most importantly such processes can help avoid, or at least reduce, the potentially disruptive impact that change can have on organizational culture.

On the other hand, transformative change always has a potentially disruptive impact on culture and this can lead to anxiety and resistance to the change within the organization's workforce. This is only natural because transformative change by its very nature induces significant transformations of one or more important elements of the organization's mission, strategies, and fundamental processes.

The Nature of Transformative Change

Transformative change in an organization is change intended to produce a transformation of one or more significant characteristics of the organization. Such transformation may be driven by any of a number of important factors in the organization's external environment, including, but not limited to, the recognition of shifting markets, the emergence of new markets, the appearance of new technologies that have a significant impact on the basic business models of the organization, changing customer needs and profiles, new government regulations, or acquisitions and mergers. By its nature, this kind of change will involve shifts in fundamental features of the organization such as business goals and objectives, underlying strategies, fundamental processes, sales cycles, and in extreme cases even the organization's mission.

The forces driving the need for shifts in fundamental features of an organization will lead to the organization feeling a certain amount of disequilibrium. In fact, the realization that the organization will succeed only if transformative changes are made can be extremely unsettling to the environment. Hence, though the associated disequilibrium is necessary in order to create a motivation for change, it is also very disconcerting to those in the organization, producing an effect that Schein [6] refers to as *survival anxiety*. Survival anxiety occurs when those in the organization become concerned or worried about the survival of the organization as it is currently configured, or perhaps its ultimate survival in any form. More personally, survival anxiety causes individuals to question such things as their future roles within the organization, whether they will add value after the organization transforms, how their position within the organization and its culture will be impacted, and indeed whether they will be needed at all after the organizational transformation is completed.

Another important feature of transformative change is that the organization is required to learn new ways of doing some of its work. In addition to the new learning that must take place, to accomplish the needed transformation something must also be *unlearned* or left behind. It can be difficult for organizations to unlearn practices and methods that may have worked over years or even decades. The combined challenge of learning something new and "unlearning" reliable and trusted practices and processes that have worked in the past can create a second major anxiety within the organization called "*learning anxiety*." High levels of learning anxiety increase the resistance to change and therefore must be managed in order for effective change to take place. Leaders in the organization must realize that the success of the envisioned transformation depends on the ability and willingness of individuals in the organization to overcome learning anxiety as they perform the learning and unlearning implicit in the transformative change process. Therefore, the sense of urgency that energizes and necessitates a transformation, must be balanced with an understanding that the process of change is complicated and cannot be done overnight.

While transformative change typically has wide organizational impact, it is important to recognize that such change does not necessarily imply a revolutionary approach, and may well be better implemented by a more deliberate evolutionary approach. As we observed in *Picasso on a Schedule*, Jim Collins in his book *Good to Great* [18] demonstrated the value of an evolutionary approach to transformative change. His study of companies that rose from good to great revealed no pattern of singularly identifiable, transforming moments to which these companies could attribute their remarkable success, but instead found evidence of the transforming impact of combining and adapting existing ideas in innovative ways. He concluded that while revolutionary leaps in results were evident, these were not achieved by the revolutionary process of embracing completely new and different ideas and concepts. Instead, he found that evolutionary, not revolutionary, processes were at work in achieving successful transformative change.

Ideally, the changes resulting from a transformation process will not appear to those in the organization as revolutionary, but will instead be viewed as innovations based on and derived from current procedures and practices through an evolutionary approach. Successful change isn't a function of whether it is revolutionary or evolutionary, but rather a function of the incorporation of new ideas and practices into the organizational structure and culture. As we will see in the following sections, an evolutionary approach that combines a compelling vision with an enabling organizational culture that embraces learning will be the most effective road to achieving long-term success through transformative change.

Compelling Vision Inspires Change

All organizations face two fundamental challenges: one short-term and one long-term. The short-term challenge is surviving within, and adapting to, the current external environment. The long-term challenge is effectively integrating internal processes to ensure the capacity to continue to survive and adapt as the external environment changes.

Vision and culture are critical to success in facing both of these challenges. In general, a compelling vision will guide the organization as it attempts to surmount both challenges, and a strong positive culture will enable the organization to weather the changes that might be needed to make the vision a reality. It is important to realize that either or both of these challenges might be surmountable through incremental change, but either or both may also require transformative change. The determining factor for which kind of change is needed will be the nature of the change in the external environment that is driving the organization's need to change.

In the case of incremental change, the vision needed will guide the organization's adaptations within the context of its current mission, its guiding principles, and its strategies. Change in some of these strategies will no doubt be required as the vision guides the organization toward a future in which it can survive, and adapt to, the changing external environment. Further changes might be required to ensure the capacity to continue to survive and adapt, and these changes could include more systemic changes to such things as organization structure, management principles and approaches, or even the composition of the workforce over time. The point is that if changes in the external environment are not too drastic, the organization may well surmount both the challenges we described through incremental change. However, even when this is the case, a guiding vision will be important to help the organization keep its equilibrium and its consensus on the goals and objectives of the changes being undertaken as well as providing a framework for managing the more specific decisions about the actual changes being implemented.

On the other hand, if the changes in the external environment are so substantial that transformative change is required to overcome either or both of these challenges, then a compelling vision becomes all the more critical to success. As we discussed in the previous section, transformative change will require the organization to not only learn something new, but to also "unlearn" something that has worked well in the past. This fact places great stress on the organization and its members materializing in the survival anxiety that we discussed earlier. This anxiety produces a state in which those in the organization come to a recognition that the organization's success will depend on undergoing significant change.

Of course recognizing that change is needed is not the same as identifying what the appropriate change is. Uncertainty about the direction and form of change then only adds to the existing survival anxiety. This increasing survival anxiety produces disequilibrium for those in the organization, and individuals will then naturally develop their own views of what is wrong and what needs to be done. Some exploration of this type may be helpful in preparing those in the organization for change, but left unchecked, this will lead to rapidly deteriorating effectiveness and the organization will fall into dysfunction as it loses its focus and spends more and more unproductive time in hand-wringing and worry.

This is the point in an organization's life where effective leadership matters the most. The leader's job is to reduce survival anxiety by refocusing the organization toward finding solutions and implementing the right kind of change to move the organization forward. Creating and articulating a compelling vision is an imperative to accomplish this. When such a vision comes from a trusted leader who has helped the organization negotiate past difficulties, it boosts morale and provides a sense of unity and determination to see the current difficulties through to a successful conclusion.

While a compelling vision is a critical catalyst to keep the stress the organization is experiencing from building to the level of dysfunction, it is important to remember that the vision alone does not resolve the underlying difficulties. For that, the organization needs an effective strategy for achieving the vision. As we described in the previous chapter, vision and strategy, while certainly related, are not one and the same.

Thus once the vision has been articulated, the organization must develop effective and achievable strategies to make the vision a reality. As noted earlier, this requires the leader to guide, but not necessarily dictate, this process. Success in this process will depend not only on a compelling vision from a trusted leader, but also the right kind of culture to enable the implementation of the strategies necessary for achieving the vision.

The Right Culture Enables Change

The challenge of transforming an organization can be directly tied to the culture of the organization. As we have noted, a significant factor that impacts the ease of transformation is the ability of the group to unlearn and relearn. If a strict adherence to existing policies and procedures has been expected and rewarded in an organization, it is doubtful that attempts to change the status quo will be received with open arms. On the other hand, a culture that includes dynamic leadership and encourages learning through self-development, freedom and responsibility is more likely to offer positive support for change.

While many observers have recognized the need for all organizations to become *learning organizations,* the achievement of this goal has proved elusive. Business organizations are focused on creating successful strategies for competing in the marketplace; there is often little time and energy left over to contemplate the challenge of how to transform the organization into a learning organization—especially when the precise definition of that term is itself elusive.

The ability of an organization as a whole to learn is related to, but different from, the notion of individual learning. In *Picasso on a Schedule,* we defined a learning organization as:

> *The Learning Organization is an ideal—a vision of what might be possible. It cannot be brought about simply by training individuals; it can only happen as a result of learning at the whole*

> *organizational level. A Learning Organization is an organiza-*
> *tion that facilitates the learning of all its members and utilizes*
> *that learning to continuously transform itself.* [1 and 19]

Peter Senge [20] has studied the concept of a learning organization extensively and asserts that a learning organization results
from a focused approached to learning that has five main features:

- Building Shared Vision

- Mental Models

- Personal Mastery

- Team Learning

- Systems Thinking

Culture plays a central role in determining the extent to which an
organization can realize the goal of becoming a learning organization. In Chapter 4, we noted that culture embodies the shared
cognitive frames—mental models, shared meanings, stories about
past successes, common understandings, linguistic paradigms—
that guide the perceptions, thought, and language used by members of the group and that are taught to new members as part of
their socialization process. Clearly culture is central then to realizing the first two of Senge's features.

In *Picasso on a Schedule,* we defined an organizational learning
model called the Paired Pyramid Model, which builds on these
underlying cultural tenets and provides a framework for realizing
the final three of Senge's features of a learning organization. The
Paired Pyramid Learning Model captures the essential elements
of how individual learning ("personal mastery" in Senge's terms)
at the conceptual or general knowledge level can be translated
through stages into actionable team and organizational learning
that can transform and renew the organization. Figure 7.1 illustrates this model.

In the Paired Pyramid Model, individual learning is accomplished at several levels through focused training and self-development programs. The first stage in individual learning is at the conceptual or general knowledge level. The concepts, principles, and techniques that apply to and help define a particular area of investigation are explored with general examples, exercises, cases, and activities illustrating the meaning and overall applicability of these concepts. This is augmented in the second stage by an exploration, guided by industry best practices, of how these concepts, principles, and techniques are interpreted and applied within the IT industry. At this level the illustrative components are replaced as appropriate with counterpart components that demonstrate the application of concepts, principles, and techniques within the context of the relevant industry best practices. In the third and final phase of individual learning, the acquired knowledge is applied to the organization's context, as ways that the knowledge and best practices might be applied within the particular organization's environment are explored.

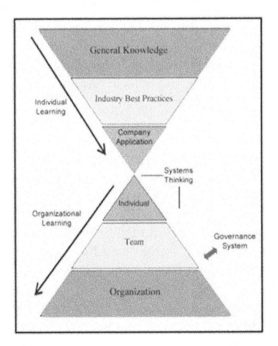

Figure 7.1: *The Paired Pyramid Organizational Learning Model.*

By the end of the three phases of individual learning, individuals should have acquired a solid conceptual foundation for the topics under consideration, insights into how and why these topics relate to industry best practices, and some specific and concrete examples of how all their new knowledge relates to their work environment. In addition, they will have been challenged to think of ways that this knowledge might modify their own perspectives, behaviors, and tasks within the organization. Note however, that thus far, no one has been asked to actually employ any of this knowledge on the job, nor has any opportunity been provided for that to happen.

Once the three phases of individual learning have been completed, individuals will return to their work environment, armed with new knowledge about some relevant topic at the conceptual, industry-specific, and organizational-specific levels. In the first phase of organizational learning, they should take up the challenge of using this knowledge to begin to modify their own perspectives, behaviors, and tasks. Note that while this may involve no one beyond the individual, it is learning within the organization setting and hence considered the first stage of organizational learning. They may in fact seek to share some of the knowledge with co-workers, but at this stage the main task is to find ways to enhance individual behavior and performance.

In the second stage of organizational learning, with the value of the newly acquired knowledge incorporated into the individual's perspective and job performance, opportunities may arise to share some of the knowledge with co-workers, managers, or those being managed. In this way, selected behaviors may be passed on to the individual's team. If a particularly good idea or technique emerges, it may be appropriate to submit suggestions for organizational change through the organization's Governance process.

In the final stage of organizational learning, the new knowledge produces modifications in the larger organization. Of course, not every individual behavior modification will make its way to this stage. Those that do will have proved their worth not just to the individual, but to teams and to the overall organization. In this stage, the use of the Governance system is essential in gaining an organizational perspective and assessment on the value of any suggested changes.

As will be clear, the individual's path from general knowledge to company-specific knowledge in the top pyramid will be taken in a much shorter time frame than the analogous path from impact on the individual's job performance to holistic organizational change. This is as it should be. But it is important to remember that improvement in individual job performance is a vital component of organizational learning and one that will be more easily implemented than changes in the processes and procedures utilized by teams and the large changes that impact the organization as a whole. Indeed, individual performance enhancement will on occasion evolve into team or organizational changes over time. The Governance process should be designed to recognize when these opportunities arise and shepherd the change process.

The organization's use of systems thinking is the glue that helps fuse individual learning and organizational learning. Figure 7.1 illustrates the crucial point at which this fusion must begin. When an individual returns from a learning experience to the workplace with new knowledge, the system or model-based view of the organization can help in the individual's assessment of the context within which any possible improvements might be made in their scope of work. The model-based view also enables an individual to be better informed when considering how these improvements might scale or relate to other interconnected parts of the organization.

The success of organizational learning is rooted in having leaders who demonstrate that they are perpetual learners themselves, and who reflect the necessity of perpetual learning at the organizational level in their vision. Such leaders will create a psychological safety net for individuals who fear the process of unlearning and relearning, reducing the learning anxiety that accompanies transformative changes. A positive, compelling vision accompanied by formal and informal training, coaching, positive role models, and systems that are consistent with the new way of thinking yield an environment that is conducive for learning and changing.

The organization that has created and nurtured a culture that encompasses a shared vision and created mental models of how the organization is to achieve that vision, that supports and expects learning by individuals, and that facilitates moving that learning to the organizational level has created the capacity to continuously *transform* itself. The organizational agility that results from the harnessing of the learning of many into a single force that is committed to the organization's objectives creates a capacity that will enable the organization to effectively implement transformative change.

Developing a Learning Culture: An Example

Once an organization has established itself as a learning organization, its culture should reflect this and if it does, it becomes the "right" culture for change. We believe that a learning culture can enhance an organization's ability to face change based on the following dimensions (adapted from Senge [20]):

- **Proactivity.** A proactive problem solving approach based on optimism, rather than a fatalistic acceptance of circumstances, characterizes a learning culture.

- **Commitment to Learning to Learn.** It is critical that organizations learn not only about changes in the external environment such as technology advances, but also about the organization itself and how it functions in a dynamic world.

- **Positive Assumptions about Human Nature.** The belief that people can and will learn and achieve when given the necessary resources and opportunities is at the heart of a learning culture.

- **Belief that the Environment Can Be Influenced.** A learning culture is one that encourages adaptation and agility in facing unexpected events and situations. Adaptive organizations are those that view change as opportunity and are willing to learn new ways of interpreting things that happen—both good and bad.

- **Commitment to Truth through Pragmatism and Inquiry.** A learning culture embraces the idea that there is no one method or source of truth and wisdom. The process of finding solutions to new or complex problems relies on an inquiry process that is flexible and dynamic, fully utilizing the knowledge of individuals in different roles.

- **Positive Orientation toward the Future.** Optimism, tied to a realistic assessment of the present, is the basis for generating the energy needed to overcome obstacles.

- **Commitment to Full and Open Task-Relevant Communication.** In order to effectively address and solve problems, organizations must have effective methods of communication for task-relevant information. Open communication and dialogue characterize a true learning environment.

- **Commitment to Diversity.** A culture that fosters diversity in thinking and innovation will enable creativity in solving new problems and dealing with new situations.

- **Commitment to Systemic Thinking.** In a complex and dynamic environment, few problems have simple linear causal solutions. Systemic thinking allows an organization to see the bigger picture, find the true sources of issues, and apply the organization's best resources to address these issues.

There are many elements or "faces" of culture as we have already noted. However, the organization that purposefully develops and nurtures its Guiding Principles can set the foundation for the culture it desires to have. In Chapter 5, we considered the I/S Division's Guiding Principles as an example of how culture can be expressed through these. A number of these Guiding Principles directly reflect the commitment of the I/S Division to Senge's dimensions of a learning culture. We revisit these below to provide a concrete illustration of how one organization has vigorously pursued the ideal of a learning organization.

Proactivity

Several of the I/S Division's Guiding Principles listed in Chapter 5 demonstrate the importance of taking a proactive stance within the I/S Division's culture.

- We are "doers". The greatest pleasure in life is doing what others say cannot be done.

- Be results oriented. This is our first operating principle. Over the long term, end results will indicate our success.

- Get the job done. Managing is not a job for the fainthearted. You will face many demanding and difficult tasks. It is up to you to utilize all the resources at your disposal to get the job done. One of your most difficult tasks will be to maintain an effective balance between control and creative solutions to problems. We must never let our control mechanisms stand in the way of delivering outstanding service to our customers.

Commitment to Learning to Learn

The I/S organization has made a significant investment in training programs that deal not only with technical subject matter, e.g., project management and systems analysis, but also in learning opportunities that focus on culture, strategy, and leadership within the organization. These programs are designed to leverage the knowledge and experiences of individuals throughout the I/S organization around topics that are critical to the organization as a whole. In addition, the organization is committed to providing individuals with the opportunity to grow on the job by offering them challenges and opportunities to stretch themselves and learn by doing. The following Guiding Principles reflect this commitment.

- o <u>Knowledge Sharing is a major form of contribution</u>. Employees are expected to continually acquire and share knowledge with other employees to increase personal value and contribute to the organization.

- o <u>We are committed to excellence</u>. In all dealings with our clients or working internally with one another, we are committed to excellence. Mediocrity and half-hearted efforts have no place in I/S. Anything less than a full commitment to excellence will erode the reputation we have worked so hard to build.

- o <u>Opportunity must be provided</u>. The truly outstanding person seeks opportunities to grow personally and professionally, to contribute, to be challenged, to achieve, to be recognized, and to advance. I/S managers must identify outstanding people and work to provide them opportunity. Put your best people on your biggest opportunities, not your biggest problems.

- o <u>Making mistakes is a sign of learning</u>. Everyone makes mistakes. It is a sign of learning as long as the same mistakes are not made again and again. Deciding when an employee is exhibiting patterns of mistakes is sometimes tough, but it must be done and corrective action must be taken.

Positive Assumptions about Human Nature

The I/S organization's attitude towards human nature is expressed in one its Three Pillars of Culture, namely that all people are given the **freedom** and **responsibility** within their assigned roles for getting the help they need from others to achieve the successful outcomes that they are accountable for. This attitude is also evident in the following Guiding Principles.

- o <u>Develop and retain outstanding people</u>. If we firmly believe that people are our most important resource, then we must build a team of truly outstanding people. Attracting, developing, and retaining these individuals is the responsibility of every manager, not only those needing more people.

- o <u>Strive for professionalism</u>. As a manager, you are responsible for developing and providing the customer with outstanding professionals who consistently maintain professional attitudes. Encourage all employees to act in a professional manner and to respect the rights and dignity of others. Anything less is unacceptable and not to be tolerated. You must be capable of leading by example.

- o <u>Competition for titles does not drive our behavior</u>. The truly outstanding person competes against the job they are given, not other employees or for titles. Compete to grow personally and professionally, to contribute, to be challenged, to achieve, to be recognized, and to advance.

- o <u>Leave the ego at the door</u>. Work as a team playing off each member's strengths and watching out for each member's weaknesses.

Belief That the Environment Can Be Influenced

Given the turbulence in the technology industry, believing that the environment can be influenced may seem unrealistic to some. However, encouraging people to seek new ways to solve problems, even when mistakes are made, fuels the belief that the environment can be influenced. The following Guiding Principles reflect this idea.

- o <u>Technology itself is never a primary cause of either greatness or decline in a business</u>. Avoid technology fads and bandwagons. Recognize that you cannot make good use of technology until you know which technology is relevant to the business it supports. Technology can accelerate business momentum, but not create it. Therefore, you need the discipline to say no to the use of technology. Crawl, walk, run is a very effective approach to technology change!

- o If you start with a blank sheet of paper, you're dead. "Thinking outside the box" has come to mean thinking of a solution that is somehow outside of what you already know and do, and coming up with something wholly new. Pushing people to think outside the box doesn't work. Instead, our approach to innovation is to take an idea or solution that has been used somewhere else, combine a number of existing ideas or solutions, and introduce them as a solution never seen before.

Commitment to Truth through Pragmatism and Inquiry

One of the underlying assumptions within the I/S culture is to always seek the truth. Several Guiding Principles capture this focus.

- o Maintain an attitude of healthy discontent. Sound management requires a probing, inquiring mind. Satisfaction with the status quo should be avoided. As you carry out your responsibilities as a manager, intelligently question existing practices and procedures. Ensure the most effective, up-to-date methods are being used. Actions based on the rationale, "that's the way we've always done it" should be examined closely. As a manager, you must not be afraid to challenge precedent. Be alert for antiquated or improper practices, which must be changed.

- o Be direct. This is an attitude. Do not mince words; question everything.

- o No excuses. Quickly admit a problem, confront it, and never be defensive.

o <u>Pay attention to detail</u>. While some organizations manage by exception, we believe this will not work in I/S. Details are necessary in order to make good decisions. As a manager, you must have these details first-hand. You cannot operate effectively with limited or second-hand information. You need facts. So how much detail is enough? As a manager, you need to know enough detailed facts to ask the right questions to help your team and to know when you hear the right answers.

Positive Orientation toward the Future

Learning that is oriented towards the near and far future is optimal. The difficulty of assessment of long-term outcomes often results in organizations focusing on learning that is geared to easy-to-assess short-term results. Learning cultures are designed to produce systemic changes in the organization that extend beyond the next quarter. In the I/S organization, assessment of programs, processes, and procedures takes place on a regular basis to ensure that they are achieving the desired results for the near-term, and tweaked if necessary for the long-term. The following Guiding Principles illustrate this approach.

o <u>Keep your eye on the goal</u>. Inventing the "Next Big Thing" is not the goal. Building the "Current Big Thing" better than anyone else *is* the goal. We are not Alpha inventors, we are Beta improvers!

o <u>Think of us as a challenger</u>. Do your job with a sense of urgency and determination. Always be attacking!

o <u>No victory laps</u>. Celebrate for a nanosecond, determine what could have been done better, and then move on!

Commitment to Full and Open Task-Relevant Communication

It is all too easy to convey large amounts of information electronically, but doing so doesn't necessarily result in effective communication. Policies that establish guidelines for the amount and type of information needed for routine tasks may help reduce information overload. A culture that fosters trust and the sharing of task-relevant information between team members is one that is less likely to face critical communication breakdowns in times of change. Several I/S Guiding Principles emphasize the importance of great communication.

- Keep the lines of communication open. Effective communication requires the flow of information up, down, and across the organization. We communicate ideas, instructions, information, and feelings. As a manager, you bear the burden for initiating and encouraging this flow.

- Practice an open door policy. We actively practice the idea of "open door" access to any level of management. Employees may ask to see any higher level of the management chain if they cannot resolve an issue with a given management level. Normally, the management chain is followed, but our policy allows for the employee to approach any level of management without disclosing the subject to the intermediate levels of management.

- Good communication is never an accident. It is the deliberate act performed through planning. Take the time to effectively communicate and ensure vital information is shared.

- Communications is the glue that binds decision-making and processes. Decision-making relies on effective delivery of specific messages designed around six components:

  - What—Key points to convey to stakeholder or group.

  - Why—A rationale for engaging them (from big picture to detailed action).

  - Who—A list of recipients to engage.

143

- When—The timing and frequency of communications.

- How—The method of delivery (face-to-face, newsletter, phone, e-mail, etc.).

- What's Next—The feedback loop: a mechanism to collect feedback, when appropriate.

  o <u>Choosing the right message and tone is vital to sending the right message</u>. Too much detail at the wrong time confuses stakeholders. Not communicating also confuses stakeholders. The proper alignment of tone and intent minimizes confusion and results in more successful communication.

  o <u>Communication is a two-way street</u>. Listening is a major part of communication. The receiver of the message must use effective techniques just like the sender.

Commitment to Diversity

Unpredictable events that result in turbulence in an organization are best addressed by the knowledge and skills of a diverse workforce. Several I/S Guiding Principles illustrate the organization's deep commitment to such diversity.

  o <u>The individual employee is important</u>. I/S managers should recognize the uniqueness of the individual. By treating people as individuals, we can release their full potential. Only then can we build a team of confident, creative people possessing a high degree of initiative and self-discipline. This results in the creation of a personally rewarding environment.

  o <u>When hiring, get the right people</u>. Place a greater weight on character attributes: work ethic, character, basic intelligence, dedication to fulfilling commitments, and ingrained values. When in doubt, don't hire – keep looking.

○ <u>Rewards are based on contribution</u>. Simple truth: The right people at any level of the organization will do the right things and deliver the best results they are capable of, regardless of the incentive system. Those employees who are best able to take advantage of the opportunities provided will receive the greatest compensation.

Commitment to Systemic Thinking

Rapidly changing technologies and business environments make it difficult to predict the direction of customer and market demands. If organizations don't have a systemic way to identify important issues and find solutions, they are likely to struggle in meeting their strategic objectives, at least in an efficient and effective manner. On the other hand, if organizations have repeatable processes as well as decision-making models for complex problems, they will be able to better address the multi-causal, nonlinear nature of such issues. The following I/S Guiding Principles reflect the importance of systemic thinking in building systems that not only meet current business needs, but also provide a foundation for future business needs.

○ <u>The best systems are built by people who understand how the systems are actually used</u>. Because we tend to develop our own code, we look for people who can think like businesspeople, which requires a lot more development and training.

○ <u>Build-it-once-for-all mentality</u>. When we write code, we automate, enhance, and change processes, incorporating logic to meet a current business need into our core systems. This provides a base to build on to meet future business needs.

○ <u>The Goal: 100% Self-Service</u>. Everyone in I/S is completely focused on how they can make our client's business easier, faster, and/or more efficient, whether the customer interaction is self-service or full-service.

- ○ <u>Do-it-yourself approach to Core Application Development</u>. We tend to manage Core Application Systems Development from programming to process engineering, which means there is no peer group support or industry best-practice knowledge from others using the same application. Therefore, we must double our efforts to find independent verification that what we develop provides a competitive operational platform for our client's business.

- ○ <u>I/S managers are first and foremost technologists.</u> In the May 20, 2002 edition of USA Today, the lead article's headline read, "Companies squander billions on tech." The article continued, "In the go-go days of the 1990s, firms spent wildly on software they really didn't need." In that same edition, the USA Today Snapshots headline was, "Technology not that important for CIO's – Only 10% of chief information officers say that technology proficiency is an important skill to be successful." The lack of proficiency in technology is why the lead headline had to be written! Our very reason for existing is the understanding of technology for the most cost-effective and efficient exploitation of that technology within the business of our clients.

- ○ <u>All costs are variable</u>. To operate a cost effective organization, we must take the view that all costs are variable over a particular time horizon and be willing to cut that cost.

Cultures and sub-cultures are unique and dynamic and dictate how an organization functions on daily tasks as well as on achieving long term strategic goals. Understanding your culture allows you to take measures to develop and enhance the positive aspects of the culture and eliminate or reduce any negative aspects that impede success.

An organization that is dedicated to learning and innovation is one that is likely to weather turbulent times by making transformative changes. Transformative changes result in organizations that don't behave like they did before, therefore a clear and compelling vision is necessary to gain the trust and confidence of individuals in the organization. The development of an organization with a culture that embraces learning is critical for individuals facing the stress and demands of unlearning and relearning their roles, processes, and procedures. The combination of strong, visionary leadership and the right culture produces an organization that is able to continuously transform itself.

Chapter 8

The Leader's Purpose

What leaders really do is prepare organizations for change and help them cope as they struggle through it.

John P. Kotter

In Chapter 3, we noted that the research of Zenger and Folkman demonstrated the nonlinear impact of effective leadership on an organization's success. Nowhere in the life of an organization is this fact more important than during periods of significant change. Indeed, Kotter [3] asserts that managers promote stability while leaders press for change, and that preparing and helping organizations through change is the very purpose of a leader.

How does the effective leader accomplish this? We believe this involves three major components:

- Prepare the organization for change
- Leverage Culture and Vision to enable change
- Lead change

In Table 3.1, there are seven attributes identified over time by the I/S organization that characterize an effective leader. These comprise the ability to:

1. Adapt to changing circumstances
2. Make a strong commitment to development
3. Clearly communicate expectations
4. Encourage and manage innovation
5. Put the right people in the right roles at the right time
6. Identify and articulate a long-term vision for the future
7. Persuade and encourage others to move in a desired direction

As we consider the three major components of how a leader prepares an organization for change and helps it cope with the change, we will see the importance of these seven leadership attributes within this process.

Preparing for Change

Recall from our Chapter 3 discussion that effective leaders invariably demonstrate *profound strengths in one or more dimensions that make a difference to their organizations.* Hence effective leaders must discover which of their strengths best fit with the needs and aspirations of the organization, then work diligently to develop those strengths to the exceptional level. In other words, before a leader can help prepare the organization for change, he or she must first prepare himself or herself to make an exceptional impact on the organization.

The first two attributes in our above list apply directly to this task:

1. *Adapt to changing circumstances*
2. *Make a strong commitment to development*

The effective leader must demonstrate the ability and willingness to adapt to changing circumstances. Demonstrating this personal agility sets an important tone for others in the organization, and helps reduce the inevitable anxieties that people will naturally feel when asked to make changes of their own. This ability to adapt to change relies to a great extent on a person's commitment to continuous improvement as demonstrated by their ongoing efforts for self-development. If the leader expects staff to make this kind of commitment, the leader's behavior must demonstrate his or her own deep commitment to this process.

In encouraging others to make such a commitment, recall that it is important to impress upon them one of the central premises of self-development: *Do Not Expect Perfection.* It is a natural human tendency to focus on others' perceptions about our weaknesses. And while we don't want to ignore those weaknesses, putting too much emphasis on them can prevent us from reaching the important goal of developing the profound strengths that optimize our potential for positive impact on the organization.

Once the leader is in the position to have an exceptional impact on the organization, how can he or she help prepare the organization for change? We believe that the major vehicle for accomplishing this is the organization's culture. Recall from Chapter 4 that culture comprises a complex blend of human behavior, attitudes, assumptions, and beliefs. And as we pointed out in that discussion, although culture is to a certain degree an abstraction, it can create significant *tangible impacts.* Indeed, culture has the power to energize and mobilize an organization toward great accomplishments, or to shackle it with unproductive and debilitating stagnation.

As Schein has noted, "culture and leadership are two sides of the same coin." In other words, it is a leader's responsibility to engage the organization in the understanding and nurturing of a culture that will support and inspire those in the organization to achieve greatness. Although interpretation of culture is always a personal thing, to create a strong energizing culture, an organization must have a clear set of *shared values and norms* that guide the way an organization actually operates. In order to be learned, culture must be experienced and then related in the individual's mind to the way the organization does its work, and learning a culture requires the kind of tacit knowledge that can come only from one's own experiences and from the advice and guidance of trusted and more experienced members of the organization.

In order to encourage a culture of shared values and norms, a leader must strive not only to embody these values and norms, but also to articulate to the organization what these are and why they are important. Of course the entire leadership team must be engaged in this process, but we should not underestimate the critical importance of each leader's own actions and words in making this process a success. As we saw in Chapter 5, there are many faces of culture, but among the most important are the organization's guiding principles, which must be lived and endorsed by the organization's leadership team.

So what kind of culture is required to help prepare the organization for change? While there are many aspects to this, we believe these can be summarized by saying that the leader should strive to create a *learning organization*. As we discussed in Chapter 7, navigating the treacherous waters of transformative change creates two categories of great anxiety in an organization. One of these is learning anxiety, which arises in all of us when we are required to learn new ways to do our work and unlearn some of the ways we have used to accomplish our work in the past. Learning anxiety is real and quite understandable. In this learning/unlearning process, an individual's standing in the organization will be challenged. The anxiety follows from worry about what our standing and our importance will be once the organization has undergone the envisioned transformation.

While learning anxiety will not disappear within the culture of a learning organization, it will not be nearly as threatening because the organization will have called on its members to learn and unlearn things all along. The concept of continuous improvement and self-development will be second nature in a true learning organization, and this gives people the confidence and reassurance that they can manage the required transformation without fear of losing their identity or being punished for temporary incompetence or uncertainty. They will be confident that the organization is set up to surmount learning challenges as it has already demonstrated through its successful experiences in doing this in the past.

The leader can draw on the middle three attributes in our list of the seven attributes of effective leaders to help minimize the inevitable disruption involved in this learning/unlearning process, namely:

3. *Clearly communicate expectations*

4. *Encourage and manage innovation*

5. *Put the right people in the right roles at the right time*

Clearly communicating expectations, even when those expectations may not be as familiar as before, provides a context that will keep people focused and help them overcome the fear derived from the question of whether they are working on the right thing or not. Of course, innovation will be required as the organization works on transformative change, and so the organization in which the leader has consistently encouraged innovation and helped create effective ways to manage it, will have a distinct advantage in achieving the appropriate innovation. Additionally, getting the right people in the right roles at the right time will be crucial for a successful organizational transformation. This will require the leader to have deep knowledge of the organization and the capabilities of the people in it. Of course, matching people to tasks is always important, but this becomes centrally important in a period of significant change. To accomplish this, leaders should know who their internal change leaders are and what their strengths and weaknesses are relative to the required change initiatives. This is the organizational equivalent of getting the right battlefield commanders in place for a difficult military campaign. The best laid strategies can go awry if this isn't done well.

Finally, the leader must recognize the potentially debilitating effect of the presence of the survival anxiety we earlier discussed when times call for significant change. Such anxiety occurs when members of the group realize that without significant change, the organization may fail outright or at the least fall into a period of significant decline. To combat the effect of this anxiety, the leader must help the organization refocus toward finding solutions and implementing the right kind of change to move the organization forward. This can only be done by creating a compelling vision for the future.

To accomplish this, the leader should draw on the last two of the seven attributes of an effective leader identified earlier:

6. *Identify and articulate a long-term vision for the future*

7. *Persuade and encourage others to move in a desired direction*

When the leader has earned the trust of those in the organization, the articulated vision will provide a direction and framework for the needed organizational change. As the leader then persuades and encourages others to move in the direction of the vision, the goal is for the organization to buy into the vision. Once this buy-in is achieved, the framework the vision offers becomes a kind of "safety net" for the organization, answering the over-riding question of "where are we going?" and freeing people up to focus on the challenges of how the organization will get there. When a compelling vision and the right learning culture are combined the organization optimizes its chances of accomplishing the transformative change that is needed for future success.

Leveraging Culture and Vision

Accomplishing transformative change is one of the most difficult challenges an organization faces. As we just discussed, one of the most important tasks leaders have is to prepare themselves and the organization for such change. We have argued that the two central elements for this are articulating a compelling vision of the future and building a strong learning culture. Once these elements are in place, they can be leveraged for success in the change process. The key to doing this is to exploit the synergies that should exist between them. Neither a compelling vision nor a strong learning culture is sufficient for the task. Ideally these will be complementary, each supporting the other in the process of transformative change. Succinctly put, vision helps align those in the organization toward a common ideal of success, and culture helps mobilize people to move effectively in the direction of that alignment.

A robust culture can provide much strength for the organization. For example, culture may encourage people to work hard, to work smart, to take risks, to demonstrate initiative, to work in teams, and so on. But before any of these cultural characteristics can be useful, the leader must set a vision and inspire people to strive for it. If a company is not aligned toward a compelling direction then problem-solving, decision-making, and iterative planning and course correction can create a black hole swallowing up immense amounts of time and energy. In this situation, the disagreements implicit in the planning and re-planning processes will consume time and other resources that should be applied to more essential activities that could advance the resolution of issues and surmounting of challenges at hand. In this kind of environment, both management and professional staff are apt to drift into cynicism and pessimism, and decision-making can degenerate into a highly politicized and polarized game.

The complexity of most modern organizations results in a workplace characterized by a high degree of interdependence. In such organizations, people do not have complete autonomy but must collaborate and work effectively together to accomplish large organizational goals. This inherent interdependence adds to the challenge of making effective organizational change. If people are not aligned to a common direction—on the "same page" so to speak—they are apt to pull in many different directions at once, resulting in a debilitating tug of war that fails to move the organization toward successful transformation. Leaders can easily fail into the trap of thinking that getting people moving in the same direction is a staff organization problem, when in fact the underlying issue is not organizational structure but lack of alignment.

On the other hand, a vision that is not within the reach of the organization's capacity cannot be realized no matter how robust the culture. A leader who vacillates on his or her vision for the organization, or does a poor job of communicating the vision, or fails to persuade people of the worthiness of the vision will not produce the alignment needed for success, no matter what capabilities the culture offers. The essential thing a compelling vision and its consequent strategies supply is a set of shared assumptions and aspirations that guide and constrain decision-making and planning, so that the expenditure of energy required in these efforts pays off in real progress toward a successful future. Organizational structure will follow the work itself once the proper work is understood and related to an overall direction.

Leading Change

Leading change is at its heart a communications challenge rather than an organizational design problem. Articulating a vision and securing the necessary organizational buy-in will invariably involve talking to many more individuals than most any other organizational challenge. The number of stakeholders involved in and affected by transformative change is typically very large. Anyone who can help implement the vision or who can hinder implementation is a stakeholder, and this includes practically the entire organization and potentially clients, customers, vendors, government regulators and others as well.

Helping people grasp and internalize a vision of an alternative future is a much more difficult communication challenge than getting them to understand the need for, and the action plan associated with, incremental change. Think of the difference between the challenge that a football coach has in communicating to his team during halftime the adjustments needed to accommodate the defensive alignment being used by the opponent in the first half of a game, as opposed to the challenge of communicating to the team a whole new offensive approach for the rest of the season after the team's quarterback has had a season-ending injury. Halftime adjustments will by their nature involve incremental change, but the second challenge will involve a significant paradigm shift in the overall way the team approaches its offense. Clearly the latter change is essentially transformative and the task of communicating the needed changes will take time, require patience, and can only be successful when these changes and the overall vision driving them are articulated clearly, convincingly, and often so that the players and other coaches who will have to implement the changes "get it" in a way that enables them to internalize the message. Only when this has happened, will the team of coaches and players be able to work through the inevitable implementation difficulties that will be encountered before a successful transformation can be attained.

Of course, understanding a message is not the same as accepting and believing the message. Thus the communication challenge of articulating a vison for the organization goes to a deeper level. To gain acceptance of an articulated vision requires that the leader have credibility. In other words, the credibility of the message will depend on the leader's inherent credibility with the people he or she is leading. As we discussed in Chapter 6, such credibility is an intangible and arises from several different sources. The main source is the trust that the leader has earned within the organization. Earned trust builds from the leader's personal integrity, experience, and deep knowledge of the organization. Experience in successfully leading change by inspiring others to follow and a deep knowledge of the organization's capacity to learn, its capabilities, and its culture are fundamental factors in earning the trust of the organization, and thus having credibility in articulating a compelling vision for the future.

Once a vision is clearly understood and truly accepted within the organization, this leads to empowerment. Empowerment allows people to move past both survival anxiety and learning anxiety to focus on forging a tangible way forward to achieve a compelling vision. Without such empowerment, people are much more apt to second guess themselves and even the vision itself because they feel powerless to move boldly in embracing the new paradigms which characterize transformative change. Empowerment comes from a clear sense of direction that has been effectively and genuinely communicated throughout the organization, and leads to employees confidently initiating actions with the assurance that their behavior is consistent with the vision.

The successful empowerment of people to act on achieving a vision cannot be achieved solely by the leader and architect of the vision. The effective leader must be able to motivate other people to provide leadership as well. For this to work, the culture must support this distributed leadership model. Such leadership across the entire organization is essential because coping with significant change in a complex organization demands initiatives from a great many people. The leader cannot possibly oversee, or even be directly involved, in all these initiatives—leaders throughout the organization, both formal and informal, must carry the flag into battle. Being able to motivate highly energized behavior is one of the leader's central responsibilities. When this is combined with direction setting which defines the path forward and alignment to get people moving down that path, the inevitable barriers to change can be overcome.

In this context, it is instructive to recall our earlier discussion in Chapter 1 about the integrated but complementary nature of the *Management* and *Leadership* systems of action.

More specifically, recall that the *Management* system of action comprises:

- A distinctive system of action to *cope with complexity*:
  - Requiring a thorough understanding of organizational structure and systems (processes) to effectively produce a degree of predictability and order

- o Utilizing the framework of processes associated with the Hierarchy and the Matrix that keep a complicated system of people and technology running smoothly
- Controlling or directing day-to-day business processes to accomplish a desired result through formal authority emanating from traditional command and control for the Hierarchy or from the authority associated with a given IT role within the Matrix.

In contrast, the *Leadership* system of action comprises:

- A distinctive system of action to *cope with change:*
  - o Requiring a set of skills and behaviors that constitute the strengths that actually define a leader and drives the *effective employment of culture and vision*
  - o Utilizing a set of processes that help direct, align, and inspire actions on the part of large numbers of people to:
    - Organize in the first place
    - Adapt their organization to significantly changing circumstances
- Guiding or inspiring other people to accomplish a desired result through *influence*

Thus, the *Management* system of action will typically employ various control mechanisms to evaluate results and compare these to what was expected, applying corrective action when a significant deviation occurs. To do this effectively, the *Management* system of action utilizes the framework of processes associated with the Hierarchy and the Matrix that keep a complicated system of people and technology running smoothly. The processes used to accomplish this should be as predictable and reliable as possible so that success does not depend on heroic actions, but can instead be achieved by the dedicated work of a determined and talented staff of normal individuals.

But this emphasis on control and reliable predictable outcomes shifts significantly when the organization is undergoing transformative change. The *Leadership* system of action then kicks in to guide and inspire people to accomplish grand visions. This requires a focus on motivation and inspiration that will (in Kotter's words) "energize people, not by pushing them in the right direction as control mechanisms do but by appealing to the basic human needs for achievement, a sense of belonging, recognition, self-esteem, a feeling of control over one's life, and the ability to live up to one's ideals." [3]

Effective leaders will motivate people by articulating the organization's vision in a manner that has credibility and makes the work seem relevant and important to the individuals receiving the message. Further, they will involve people in deciding *how* to achieve the organization's vision, giving them a sense of ownership in the outcome as well as a feeling of some control over how the outcome will be achieved. In this process, effective leaders will motivate and encourage people by providing coaching and mentoring, by being powerful role models, and by recognizing and rewarding exemplary efforts and achievement, thus helping people develop professionally and enhancing their self-esteem and commitment to the long-term future of the organization.

Part V
Applying the Art and Science of Leadership

Chapter 9

The Hierarchy and Matrix Leadership Cycles

The underlying theme of this trilogy of books is: *The Art and Science of Managing IT.* Throughout the series we have stressed that IT is a discipline and an industry that demands both art and science for success. The mix of art and science differs significantly depending on the nature of the challenges being faced, and also as one moves between the *Management* and *Leadership* systems of actions. Leadership is surely based on many intangibles, and therefore the effective leader will certainly need to master as much art as science in its practice.

To learn to lead depends on the direct experience and personal knowledge that comes from intimate contact with others who understand the art and science of leadership. The fact is this type of intimate contact has become more difficult to achieve as organizations have grown larger and become more diversified. To be a truly effective leader, one must find ways to overcome this difficulty of gaining experience and personal knowledge.

Recall in Chapter 1 of this book two types of leadership were defined as essential categories of leadership within the IT OSD Model:

- Hierarchical Leadership which has the responsibility of *efficiently using the organization's resources: human, financial, and other* to ensure the *Matrix produces client value-based outcomes,* and

- Matrix Leadership which has the responsibility for *effectively using the organization's human and other resources in the competent and timely completion of excellent work to produce the client value-based outcomes.*

The Hierarchy Leadership Cycle

One way to overcome the difficulty of gaining personal knowledge through direct intimate contact with those who understand the art and science of leadership is through a set of repeatable processes for leadership, referred to as cycles, which have been defined and utilized by the I/S Division for each type of leadership within the IT-OSD Model. The first cycle shown in Figure 9.1 supports the development of Hierarchy Leadership.

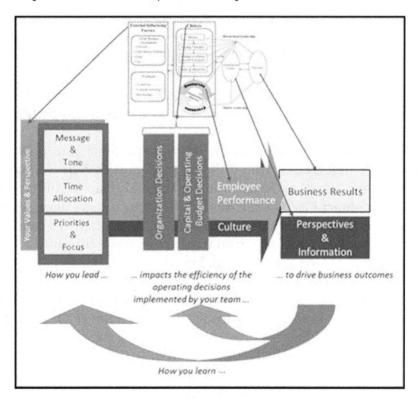

Figure 9.1: *The Hierarchy Leadership Cycle*

The Hierarchy Leadership Cycle is focused on the Hierarchy's key challenge of *ensuring the work gets done* relative to the objectives of cost, time, and quality. It has the following features:

- The foundation for this Cycle is the perspectives and values of the individual within the Hierarchy which is critical to the IT organization's success. An individual's perspectives are gained from understanding External Influencing Factors, the Strategies to influence these factors, and the System Architecture (See Chapter 2). An individual's values are influenced through an understanding, acceptance, and application of organizational values shared through its culture (See Chapter 5).

- The basis for how an individual within the Hierarchy leads is dependent on their leadership competencies and the development of their profound strengths which are discussed in detail in Chapter 3. In addition there are tasks associated with leadership competencies which are critical to leadership:

  ○ One such task is *communication* accomplished through the use of interpersonal skills to find the right message and tone.

  ○ Another task is *determining the correct priorities and focus* which is accomplished through resource planning and management and involves the leader's own time allocation to the best tasks to achieve successful outcomes.

- Within the IT-OSD Model there are choices identified that must be made by the Hierarchy for the IT organization. These choices have direct influence on any organizational, capital, and operating budget decisions made by individual leaders acting within this leadership cycle. The decisions made will impact the efficiency of the execution of the processes defined within the Rainbow Chart of Processes.

- Research has shown that the leadership provided by the individual within the Hierarchy has a significant impact on *employee performance* as well as *client satisfaction* (See Chapter 3).

- It is also important to realize that each execution of this Cycle has an impact on the building and nurturing of the IT organization's culture. When done correctly, executing this cycle helps build and re-enforce the culture slowly over time. When done badly, it can destroy culture in an instant.

- As with any effective cycle, there are feedback loops which when used correctly can help an individual within the Hierarchy become a better leader. As this happens, they become more effective in running IT as a successful business.

The Matrix Leadership Cycle

The Matrix Leadership Cycle is focused on the Matrix's key challenge of *getting the work done* relative to the objectives of cost, time, and quality. This cycle is shown in Figure 9.2.

The Matrix Leadership Cycle has the following features:

- The foundation for this Cycle is the character, capability, and motivation of the individual leaders within the Matrix. Employing and developing people who excel in these attributes is critical to the IT organization's success. The foundation is supported by their actions and behaviors—meaning what others see—which should be influenced through an understanding, acceptance, and application of organizational values shared through the IT organization's culture (See Chapter 5).

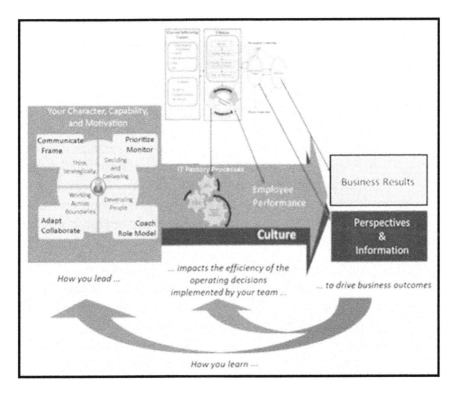

Figure 9.2: *The Matrix Leadership Cycle*

- Just as is true for leaders in the Hierarchy, the basis for how individual leaders within the Matrix lead is dependent on their leadership competencies and the development of their profound strengths which are discussed in detail in Chapter 3.

- In addition, individual leaders within the Matrix should learn and apply the following processes which define what a Matrix Leader actual does to be successful:

  o **Develop People**: Leaders develop people with different approaches based upon the skills and motivation of the team member, the nature of the task, and the time available. Coaching is a critical tool to effectively develop a person which was described in detail within *Managing Picasso*, Chapter 6.

○ **Work across Boundaries**: Cultivating and maintaining a network of relationships is a vital asset to a Matrix Leader. It is important to note that there are different levels of stakeholder relationships and each should be managed differently. Management of these relationships requires conscious focus and nurture. Matrix Leaders need to balance advocacy with inquiry when communicating with stakeholders and recognize that communication is an essential skill in relationship building.

○ **Think Strategically**: Leaders focus activity for themselves and others. They focus through specific goals and direction, through a vision of what is to be viewed as successful, and through framing what should be done and what should not be done. Strategic thinking requires different skills at different levels within an IT organization. Framing is one of the most powerful tools of strategic leadership. Matrix Leaders tend to create narrow frames to help focus and drive action.

○ **Decide and Deliver**: Matrix Leaders deliver results through prioritization, decision making, and accountability. It is critical for Matrix Leaders to continuously evaluate and manage priorities based on the outcomes which must be delivered. Matrix Leaders manage a cycle of accountability from the beginning of the work assignment through feedback after the work assignment is completed. As an effective role model for others, Matrix Leaders should hold themselves accountable and take personal responsibility for the decisions made and the results obtained.

• Within the IT-OSD Model, Matrix Leaders are responsible for the execution of the processes defined within the Rainbow Chart of Processes. The successful execution of these processes is based on each individual leader within the Matrix understanding of how these processes work and the correct application of the processes which impacts the effectiveness of the processes.

- As is the case for Hierarchy Leaders, research shows that the leadership provided by an individual within the Matrix has a significant impact on *employee performance* as well as *client satisfaction* (See Chapter 3).

- Once again, each execution of this Cycle has an impact on the building and nurturing of the IT organization's culture. When done correctly execution of such cycles helps build and re-enforce the culture slowly over time. When done badly, it can destroy culture in an instant.

- Finally, there are feedback loops within the Matrix Leadership Cycle, which are there to help the individual Matrix Leader gain deeper insight into the working of the processes within the Rainbow Chart of Processes as well as becoming a better leader of the people engaged in the execution of those processes.

Learning through Leadership Simulations

In addition to a set of repeatable processes for leadership, the I/S Division, working with Nick Noyes, Founding Partner, Insight Experience, Inc., has developed a set of training simulations to help provide direct experience in leading while under the watchful eyes of those who understand the art of leadership. Each simulation provides a participant:

- An immersion experience, with reflection

- A parallel business environment in which to apply, practice and integrate

- Time compression to see the short- and long-term impacts of decisions being made

- An opportunity to compare approaches and results among simulation teams

- An introduction to working and learning cross-organizationally

- A platform for interpersonal and team feedback

In the simulation developed to support Hierarchy Leaders, a team of five to six participants collectively assumes the role of the General Manager of a fictional company couched as an independent business unit within a larger company. The simulation presents the team–the new General Manager–with a variety of strategic leadership issues and challenges. Each team makes business decisions over three to four rounds. After each round, the teams receive a business debrief and feedback on the simulated performance of company for which they are responsible.

This business simulation exercise challenges the team to effectively apply their leadership skills using the Hierarchy Leadership Cycle, and enables them to see the impact of their leadership decisions on the simulated business. As it progresses, the simulation allows participants to gain intimate, first-hand experience on:

- Setting direction and communicating that direction to reinforce the strategic priorities of the overall organization

- Recognizing the unique objectives and goals of each business function

- Managing the business unit within a quarterly budget that is provided while making budget related decisions for each business function and achieving pre-defined performance objectives

- Managing time by determining how the General Manager should spend their time by allocating it over 8 different activities

- Enabling projects by identifying, evaluating and endorsing projects based on cost, benefit, and support of business strategy

- Engaging special and product projects designed to push the organization forward

- Dealing with issues which are an opportunity, challenge, or problem that is specific to and must be solved within a single quarter.

A second simulation was developed to support Matrix Leaders. During this program, the challenges and opportunities facing frontline Matrix Leaders are explored and best practices for success are introduced. The simulation exercise challenges each participant to effectively apply their leadership skills using the Matrix Leadership Cycle, and enables them to see the impact of their leadership decisions on the simulated business outcomes. The simulation allows participants, while under the watchful eye of experienced leaders supporting the simulation, to gain intimate, first-hand experience on:

- Communicating a strategic message

- Adjusting to changing timelines

- Managing peers

- Allocating time

- Delegating work

- Handling customer complaints

- Managing key stakeholders

- Resolving cross-organizational issues

- Addressing conflicting organizational priorities.

During the simulation, each participant works with a team to make decisions over three to four rounds. Each round has several issues for each team to consider and make decisions on how to address. After each round, each team receives progress reports on project results (progress toward deadline, budget and quality), team member development, and leader development. At the conclusion of the program each participant will be better able to:

- Think strategically to prioritize actions and set clear direction

- Lead and manage the work of a team in a matrix organization to deliver results

- Coach and develop people to improve motivation and performance

- Communicate effectively up, down and across in an organization

Given today's large, diversified business environment, we believe the most efficient and effective way to become a successful leader is through intimate contact with others who understand the art and science of leadership. This can be done through an integrated education program that teaches the set of repeatable processes, explains the use of Leadership Cycles, and provides rigorous simulation experiences like those described above. Taken together these efforts provide members of the Hierarchy and Matrix Leadership teams the opportunity to learn fundamental concepts, then practice the execution of activities required to be a successful leader in a controlled environment in which immediate feedback is made available to improve an individual's leadership performance.

Chapter 10

A Case Study in Transformative Change

We believe that being an effective leader in an IT company depends on an understanding and mastery of a set of well-defined and interconnected principles that enable and energize great IT leadership. These principles comprise the foundation for creating a compelling and authentic *vision* and for building and sustaining a *culture* that provides the agility and underlying strength to maintain success in achieving that vision in the face of the rapid, often unpredictable, and potentially disorienting change that characterizes the IT industry.

As we conclude the writing of this book, the I/S Division of BlueCross BlueShield of South Carolina is in the midst of transformative change. In this chapter, we will describe the drivers and nature of this change and highlight how the organization is making essential use of many of the central concepts described in this book to address the challenges associated with the required change.

Change Drivers

Recall the IT-OSD Model introduced briefly in Chapter 1 of this book and discussed at some length in Chapter 3 of *Picasso on a Schedule*. This model, illustrated in Figure 10.1, provides a framework for making the necessary environmental scans—both internal and external—to assess the overall health of the organization and take an analytical approach to continuous evolutionary adaptive change. As shown here, the IT-OSD model has three main component groups: External Influencing Factors, Organizational Choices, and impacts of these choices in the form of Culture and Outcomes achieved. As an organization responds and adapts to new environmental challenges, the model helps the organization consider the most important interconnections and interdependencies that are inherent in any complex organizational system, enabling the organization to take these interconnections and interdependencies into account when design choices are made.

External Influencing Factors will, of course, vary over time. While the organization may have little or no direct control over these influences, it can nevertheless make design choices that help to accommodate the impact of these external factors relative to the organization's ability to achieve its desired outcomes. Note that the IT-OSD model groups important External Influencing Factors for an IT organization into two broad categories: the *Client Business Environment* and the *IT Industry*. Each of these categories represent outside elements that directly affect the nature of the results created by an IT organization.

Within this structure, the model provides a framework to ask, and the awareness to provide reasoned answers to, questions like the following: What new challenges are our clients and their customers likely to face in the future? How are our competitors positioned to respond to these challenges? What weaknesses in our current products and services are likely to be exposed by these evolving challenges? What IT industry realities and best practices will impact our processes, products, and services? How can these realities and best practices be accommodated to make our organization stronger and better positioned for future success?

In order to utilize the IT-OSD Model appropriately, the IT organization must work within the context of running IT as a business which has been discussed at length within both the books *Picasso on a Schedule* and *Managing Picasso*. The important point to remember here is that an IT organization could be a 'business within a business' or a standalone business within the IT Industry itself. This differentiation was originally developed based on the way the U.S. Bureau of Labor Statistics defined IT as both an IT organization within the distinct industry of IT and a subset of Manufacturing, Transportation, Insurance, Business Services and other business industries and sectors in which an IT organization operates.

Over the past several years, two important change drivers for the I/S Division have emerged—one from each of the Client Business Environment and the IT Industry categories (shaded in Figure 10.1) —within the External Influencing Factors component of the IT-OSD Model. Each of these have presented challenges to the I/S Division that require significant change.

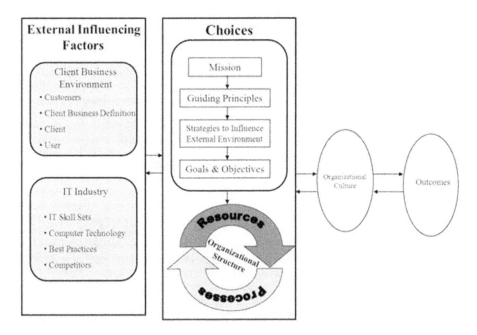

Figure 10.1: *The IT-OSD Model: External Influencing Factors*

The Client Business Environment within which the I/S Division's 'business within a business' model resides is *healthcare insurance/ payer processing.* The change driver that has emerged from the

Client Business Environment is a strong trend toward placing management of services and execution of Application Systems in support of a given client within cost-effective, highly secure, and advanced technical infrastructure environments referred to as *data centers*. This trend can be clearly seen in the movement of consolidating Application Systems used to support the administrative processes, and of consolidating data centers that supported those Application Systems within the programs administered by the Centers for Medicare and Medicaid Services, a federal agency within the United States that administers the Medicare program. This change driver presented an opportunity to leverage the I/S Division's physical assets and experience in running data centers to allow BCBSSC to enter the *Data Center Hosting* business.

The second major change driver has emerged within the IT Industry category of External Influencing Factors. Over the past few years, *Cloud Services* has emerged as an important new development within the Data Center Hosting business. Hence, once BlueCross BlueShield of SC entered the Data Center Hosting business, the Cloud Services business presented a possible new major business opportunity that needed to be considered.

The Vision for Change

In analyzing the challenges to the I/S Division that were created by the two change drivers emanating from the External Influencing Factors described above, two major questions arose each of which required a visionary answer.

Let's first consider the major change driver that arose within the Client Business Environment. The I/S Division decided that the most promising way to successfully take advantage of the opportunity to enter the Data Center Hosting business depended on the creation of a subsidiary company called Companion Data Services which reported into the I/S Division. Through Companion Data Services (CDS), the I/S Division is now a major provider of hosting services for the healthcare insurance industry, especially for government insurance programs such as Medicare. However, this single event forced the I/S Division to rethink the 'business within a business' model by addressing the following central question:

When an IT company, which utilizes the 'business within a business' model to serve clients in a non-IT industry, creates a subsidiary which is itself an IT company operating within the larger IT industry, should the subsidiary still be treated as a client within the 'business within a business' model?

In other words, should the subsidiary be viewed as another client by the parent IT company? If so, how does this type of client, operating in the larger IT Industry, differ (if at all) from clients who operate in a non-IT Industry? These questions were resolved utilizing the following analysis.

- The I/S Division's 'business within a business' model utilized a process framework (the Rainbow Chart of Processes) that provided a set of clearly defined, integrated, repeatable, and highly successful processes for interacting with the client organizations that it supported. However, in dealing with CDS, a client organization which is itself in the IT Industry—but which is also a part of the I/S Division utilizing services from the I/S Division—the clarity of responsibility within the repeatable process framework became blurred. So the question arose: How should the 'business within a business' model be utilized by the I/S Division when dealing with CDS?
  - The ITIL Diagram, Version 2, shown in Figure 10.2 was revisited with the focus on thinking about what is shown in the diagram as 'The Business'. This was done in conjunction with a deep re-examination of the Rainbow Chart Processes associated with 'The Business Perspective' as it related to I/S Division non-IT clients and the subsidiary CDS.

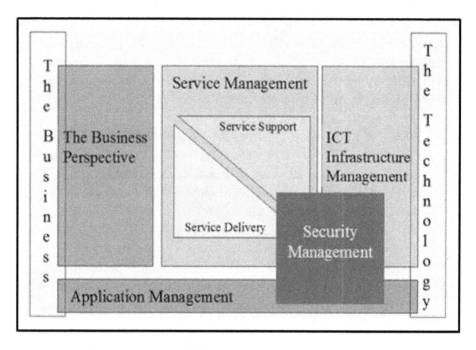

Figure 10.2: *The ITIL Diagram, Version 2*

○ After much deliberation, a new vision was formed that encompassed more precise definitions for the interactions between 'The Business' and 'The Business Perspective' components of the ITIL Framework and the processes that support these interactions. This new vision demonstrated that in fact there is *no essential difference* in the way an IT organization should deal with a client organization within a non-IT industry or a client organization within an IT business within the IT industry. In other words, the IT organization should always operate in the 'business within a business' model.

○ The implementation strategy for this vision will be discussed in the next section.

Let's now consider the second major change driver. This change driver emerged within the IT Industry category of External Influencing Factors, and revolved around a new business opportunity for the Division's subsidiary Companion Data Services in the Cloud Services business. The I/S Division's basic capabilities and the experience of CDS in operating complex data centers seemed to position the I/S Division to consider entering the evolving and expanding Cloud Services business. However, any serious consideration of doing so required the answer to the following central question:

> *What area within the Cloud Services business would best fit the I/S Division's distinctive capabilities, and once this has been identified, could the I/S Division's offerings in this area be differentiated from the competition within the Cloud Services market in a way that could create a sustainable competitive advantage?*

In other words, what strategies would be needed to leverage the expertise and experience that CDS has in operating large data centers to produce competitively distinctive services in the Cloud Services market. These questions were resolved utilizing the following analysis.

- As a first step in trying to identify an opportunity to offer truly differentiated cloud services, the I/S Division utilized the existing Research & Development process of the Rainbow Chart of Processes, to gain an understanding of the Cloud Computing Services marketplace and the Cloud Service Providers (CSPs) who were competitors already established within this marketplace. Once this understanding was gained, I/S and CDS could begin the search for potentially differentiating capabilities.

  - The detailed study of the Cloud Service Providers (CSPs) and their marketing message as well as the actual services they provided to the marketplace revealed some encouraging possibilities. First, the study found that

CSPs promised Client IT organizations that they would be able to focus on projects that differentiate *their business*, rather than focusing on running and maintaining data centers—a very attractive proposition. However, the study revealed that the reality was that the Client IT organizations actually had to fill in a substantial number of functions related to running and maintaining data centers which were not provided by the CSPs! This information is summarized using the applicable portions of the Rainbow Chart of processes shown in Figure 10.3. (Note: The Rainbow Chart excerpts shown here and in Figure 10.4 are based on an *updated version* of the Rainbow Chart which is shown in full later in this chapter in Figure 10.13.)

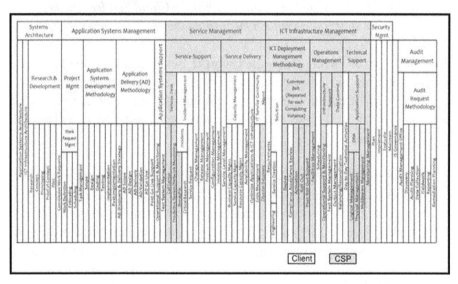

Figure 10.3: *Illustrating Client and CSP Responsibilities*

○ Using this information a vision was created to differentiate the CDS offering from competitors by filling the gaps in function not provided by CSPs through a set of unique highly scalable processes referred to as *Managed Cloud Services* (MS). The CDS offering would then allow a client's IT organization to truly focus on what differentiates their business and not on running data centers as Figure 10.4 illustrates.

o The impact of this analysis and the vision to create a set of Managed Cloud Services is that I/S and CDS could differentiate its Cloud Services offerings by filling a large and essential gap between what the current CSPs promise and what they actually deliver.

o The implementation strategy for this vision will be discussed in the next section.

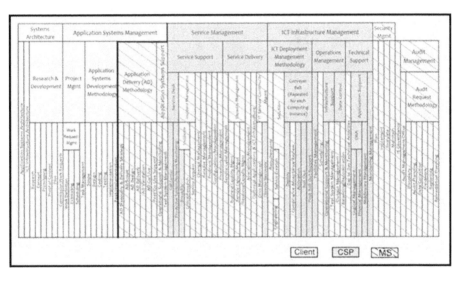

Figure 10.4: *Illustrating Client, Managed Services (MS), and CSP Responsibilities*

From Vision to Strategy

As noted earlier in this book, a vision is not the same as a strategy. The effective leader will realize this and focus on communicating the vision in a compelling way, motivating others to want to achieve the vision, and then seeking input from other strategic leaders in the organization to devise strategies to accomplish the vision.

Of course, the aim of any new strategy is to create modified Outcomes that will produce the new value that clients envision. As Figure 10.5

illustrates, in the IT-OSD Model Outcomes are produced by combining Resources and Processes utilizing an appropriate Organizational Structure and working within the Culture of the organization.

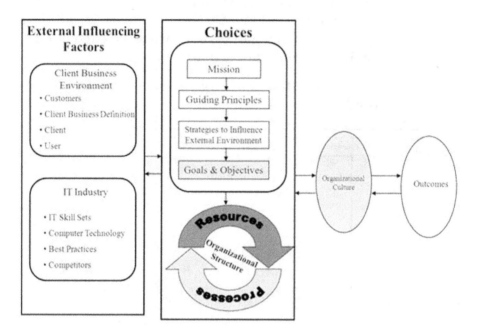

Figure 10.5: *The IT-OSD Model: Achieving Outcomes*

At the heart of this overall ability to achieve the desired Outcomes is a set of Processes that the organization has chosen as a framework for its work. In Chapter 2, we described the Hierarchical Matrix Organizational Structure and its associated Rainbow Chart of Processes. In devising strategies to accomplish the visions described above, it seems natural that the organization would use the Rainbow Chart of Processes as a guide about changing appropriate processes to ensure those Outcomes. This is exactly what the I/S Division has done for the two transforming changes we described earlier.

Recall that the Rainbow Chart of Processes represents processes broken into the Nine Major Process Groups of IT. For reference, we have reproduced here the Nine Major Process Groups in Table 10.1 and the Rainbow Chart of Processes with refinements in Figure 10.6 as it was configured *before the current change initiatives began.*

Table 10.1

Fundamental IT Processes and Process Groups with Example First-Level Refinements (before change initiatives)

IT Process Framework

Adaptive Change Process Group — 1. **Adaptive Change**
  i. IT Governance
  ii. Quality Assurance

2. **Line of Business Management**
  i. Financial Management
  ii. Resource Acquisition

3. **Enabling Processes**
  i. Managing People Program
  ii. Administrative Tasks

Business Perspective Process Group (The Hierarchy)

4. **Client Management**
  i. Relationship Management
  ii. Steering Support (Client Work requests)
  iii. Product Improvement
  iv. Systems/Service Monitoring
  v. Internal Marketing

5. **System Architecture**
  i. Application Systems Architecture
  ii. ICT Infrastructure Architecture

6. **Application Systems Management**
  i. Project Management
  ii. Research & Development
  iii. Application System Development & Maintenance
  iv. Application System Support

System Factory Process Group (The Matrix)

7. **Service Management**
  i. Service Support
  ii. Service Delivery

8. **ICT Infrastructure Management**
  i. Infrastructure Deployment Management
  ii. Operations Management
  iii. Technical support

9. **Security and Audit Management**
  i. Information Security Management
  ii. Audit Management

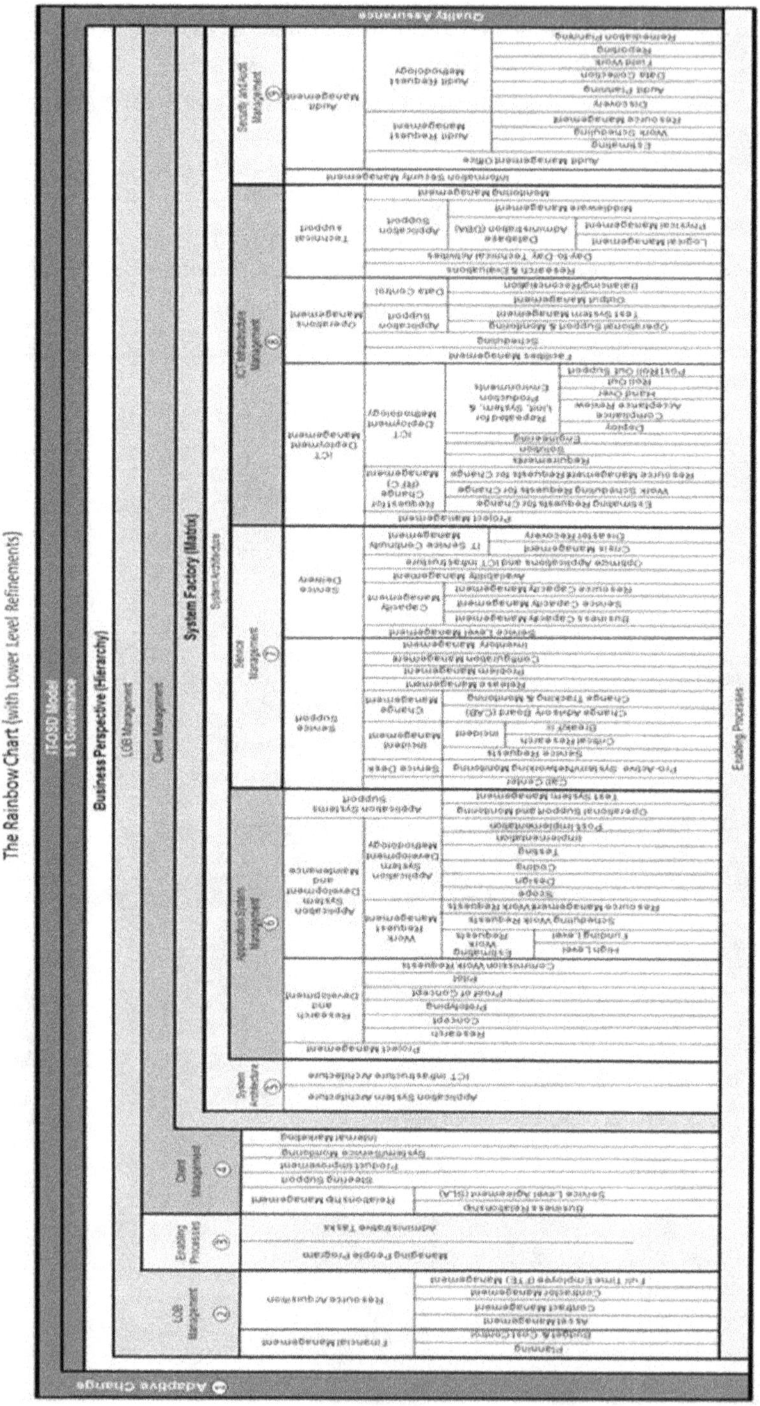

Figure 10.6: *The I/S Division Rainbow Chart of Processes (as of December 2014) with Lower-level Refinements*

'The Business' and 'The Business Perspective' ITIL Components

In dealing with the vision that an IT Organization should always operate in the 'business within a business' model, the I/S Division implemented a new strategy that encompassed implementing more precise definitions for the interactions between 'The Business' and 'The Business Perspectives' components of the ITIL Framework and the processes that support these interactions.

These new definitions and processes which described the needed Client Business processes for interaction with the Rainbow Chart of Processes are shown in Figure 10.7. An important distinction to note is that this set of Client Business processes is not a component of the I/S Rainbow Chart of Processes, but instead resides *within the Client Business* to facilitate the client's ability to effectively interact with the Rainbow Chart of Processes.

In other words, these newly articulated definitions and processes provide the needed clarity and consistency in the responsibilities of *all client types* and their interactions with the I/S Rainbow Chart of Processes as it creates value-based Outcomes for its clients. This clarity and consistency was particularly needed around the activities and responsibilities of the client versus the IT organization in:

- Defining the scope and requirements for IT work efforts needed to support a client's business

- Client project management activities and responsibilities versus IT organization project management activities and responsibilities

- Customer management activities and responsibilities versus Client Management activities and responsibilities within the IT organization

- Client financial management activities and responsibilities versus LOB Financial Management activities and responsibilities within the IT organization

- Client security and compliance activities and responsibilities versus IT organization activities and responsibilities in these areas.

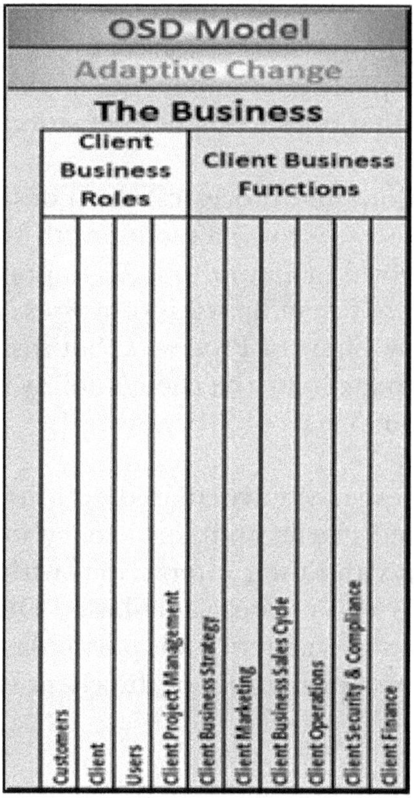

Figure 10.7: *The Client Business Processes Needed to Interact with the I/S Rainbow Chart Processes*

Following are the definitions of the processes for which *all client types are responsible.*

The OSD Model: Organizational System Design Model, introduced by Paul Gustavson to help business organizations better evaluate and understand the connections between various organizational design factors as they seek to achieve a design that will produce outcomes that support their strategic goals.

Adaptive Change: The Adaptive Change Component recognizes the need for a process to allow for innovation and adaptation within a Business organization's administrative and operational areas.

The Business. An individual or entity, which the IT organization will refer to as a *client,* engaged in commerce, manufacturing, or a service that requires the use of IT services in an attempt to make surplus income (a profit) for distribution to its owners or to uses its surplus revenues to further achieve its purpose or mission in the general good of society, rather than distributing its surplus income.

Client Business Roles

The Client Business utilizes four major roles as follows:

1) **Customer**

   A person or business that purchases a commodity or service offered by a particular client.

2) **Client**

   A person within a client's business who is:

   • Authorized to conclude an agreement with the IT organization about the provision of IT services

   • Responsible for remuneration of IT services provided.

3) **User**

   A person who uses IT services for their routine activities as related to the client's business; the person who's 'hand is on the keyboard'. Customers, clients, and client employees can play the role of the user.

4) **Client Project Manager**

   A person who employs processes related to planning, organizing, staffing, directing and controlling *client business activities* which must be executed to ensure that project work is delivered on time, within budget, adheres to high quality standards, and meets *customer expectations.*

Client Business Functions
Comprises a set of six processes (shown in Figure 10.7 and described below) that define the buying and selling of goods and services by a particular client in support of their customers in the form of short and long range plans, financial plans, organizational structures, business practices, operations and administrative processes.

Client Business Strategy
Processes related to long range product and financial planning, organizing, staffing, directing, and controlling of the client business.

Client Marketing
Processes related to continuously adding value to the client business by conducting market analysis and making strategic and innovative recommendations regarding the brand management (including tools, tone, and messaging) approach necessary to engage current and prospective customers and position the business as a trusted resource.

Client Business Sales Cycle
Processes related to a Clients Business Sales Cycle which is utilized for all new business opportunities, including business expansions and change orders. The processes could be direct sales or custom, bid type sales. In a bid type sale process, the steps follow a general flow of Pursue, Fit, Bid/Modification (New Business or Change orders on existing business), Submit, and Post-Submittal.

Client Operations
Processes related to a particular client business supporting their customers in the form of tactical planning and ongoing operational activity related to the goods or services being supplied to the customer.

Client Security and Compliance
Processes related to:

- Defining the needed level of security for a client's business taking into consideration internal requirements, as well as external contractual or legal requirements and establishing the appropriate Service Level Agreements (SLAs)

- Monitoring and evaluating security-related activities, policies, procedures and controls needed to determine if they are being adhered to in an effective and efficient manner; and to identify opportunities for improvement

Client Finance
Processes to manage a client business organization's budgeting, accounting and resource acquisition.

Based on the experience of the I/S Division, the authors believe that every IT organization should always operate in the 'business within a business' model even when it is supporting a standalone IT business within the IT Industry. This is because this model naturally forces the interactions of efficiency and effectiveness which results in value-based outcomes, as has been described previously in *Picasso on a Schedule* and *Managing Picasso*.

Differentiating Managed Cloud Services in the Marketplace

To deal with the new vision to differentiate the CDS Cloud Service offerings from competitors by filling the gaps in function not provided by CSPs, the I/S Division pursued a strategy of developing and then implementing a set of unique highly scalable processes referred to as *Managed Cloud Services* (MS) that would allow a client's IT organization to truly focus on projects that differentiate their business and not on running data centers.

The research into the Cloud Computing market noted earlier, resulted in the I/S Division and CDS not pursuing Self-Service Cloud Computing Offerings, because it was decided that there was no way to create unique differentiation from competitors in this space. However, this research also showed that differentiation could be achieved by providing the processes that filled the gaps in function not provided by competitors within the Self-Service space. Two types of offerings were identified for implementation:

- The first is referred to as **Managed Services.** In this service model, CDS would fill *most of the gaps* in cloud computing services offered within a Cloud Service Providers (CSPs) Data Center.

- The second is referred to as **Managed Services Plus.** In this service model, CDS would fill *all the gaps* in the cloud computing services offered within a CSP Data Center because *Managed Services Plus* is offered in data centers completely under the control of CDS which allows for all known gaps to be filled.

The central strategy within these offerings was to leverage a standard set of processes related to Information Communication Technology (ICT) Infrastructure deployment that had already been developed by the I/S Division in support of the CDS Hosting business. The standard set of processes was used to create, as far as is known, the first and only standard Deployment Management Methodology (DMM) for ICT Infrastructure. The DMM is a conceptual model used in project management that describes the stages involved in an ICT Infrastructure development and deployment work effort to support a software system(s), from initial Scope of Work Definition through Post-Implementation as well as Maintenance of the deployed ICT Infrastructure. Documentation is crucial and is done in parallel with the deployment process.

The DMM process was integrated into the Rainbow Chart of Processes under the major process described in the ITIL framework as ICT Infrastructure Management and within the I/S Division's sub-process: ICT Deployment Management Methodology (DMM). This sub-process, shown in the excerpt from the Rainbow Chart of Processes in Figure 10.8, represents the Design and Planning and the Deployment processes defined within the ITIL Framework.

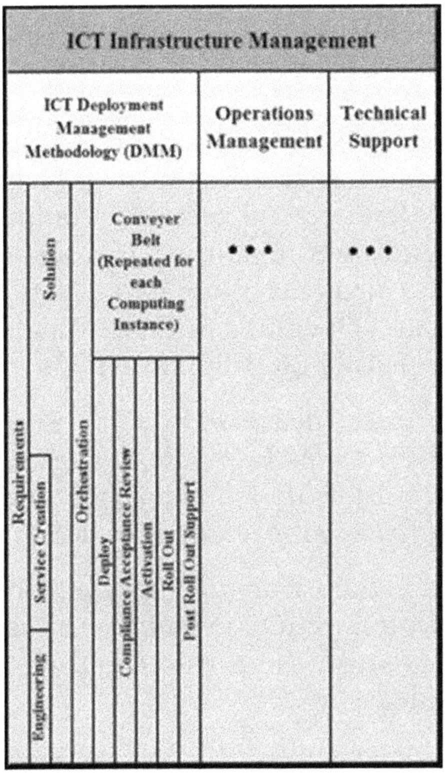

ICT Infrastructure Management		
ICT Deployment Management Methodology (DMM)	Operations Management	Technical Support
Requirements / Service Creation: Engineering / Solution: Orchestration — Conveyer Belt (Repeated for each Computing Instance) / Deploy / Compliance Acceptance Review / Activation / Roll Out / Post Roll Out Support	• • •	• • •

Figure 10.8: *The ICT Deployment Management Methodology Sub-Process within the I/S Rainbow Chart*

Having a standard methodology that supports the development, deployment, and maintenance of ICT Infrastructure is a fundamental requirement to achieve consistency and quality, but high scalability through automation within the processes had to be achieved to provide a solid differentiating factor for CDS. So the next step in implementing this strategy was to develop and implement automation within the processes. Again, the initial research into this strategy was accomplished using the existing Research & Development process of the Rainbow Chart of Processes. The solution to this strategy was the development and implementation of what is referred to in the Cloud Computing world as a Unified

Control Plane to manage all ICT Infrastructure Solutions across multiple data centers. This was accomplished by:

1. Focusing on how x86, UNIX, z/Series, Storage, and Network Hardware and Software are similar (as opposed to focusing on their differences) in terms of Compute, Storage, and Network, and then organizing thousands of IT hardware and software elements by use into a Master Index comprising: Hardware, Operating Systems, Middleware, Databases, Development Tools, ICT Support Tools

2. Creating pre-designed Infrastructure Service Offerings for Computing Platforms: Compute, Storage, and Network using elements from the Master Index and then storing them in the Service Catalog for reuse in the design step of the DMM

3. Utilizing the Infrastructure Designer Tool developed by the I/S Division to initiate and control the Design step of the DMM to satisfy the requirements of given Application System Software by:

   a. Designing the infrastructure solution through selecting the Service Offerings that can support the software requirements

   b. Readying the infrastructure solution for deployment by selecting from the Component Catalog pre-engineered Computing Platform Models which identify the components that are authorized to fulfill given IT Hardware or Software elements within a Service Offering to include hardware model or software version

4. Initiating the deployment step of the DMM though the Infrastructure Designer Tool feeding data into commercially available Cloud Orchestration software that identifies, reserves, and then deploys actual assets either:

   a. Virtually—by sending instructions through appropriate scripting to element managers on the required hardware to deploy the solution, or

    b. Physically—by creating build instructions through the same appropriate scripting to deployment specialists who physically deploy the solution through a standardized conveyor belt process

5. Creating and maintaining audit records associated with every deployed solution

6. Collecting meaningful utilization data on every deployed solution

The implementation of this strategy resulted in the development and implementation of a set of unique highly scalable processes supported by an integrated highly automated system. This system, referred to as the *Integrated Cloud Orchestration System* (ICOS), includes the Infrastructure Designer, the Cloud Orchestrator, as well as other functions to support the daily operation of the ICT Infrastructure, Break-Fix, and Maintenance Processes.

A basic assumption in automating the DMM process was that the ICT Infrastructure requirements for a given Application System were readily obtainable from the software developers/maintainers. This assumption turned out not to be true. In fact, the software developers/maintainers were not aware of much of the information required to create a production/test infrastructure environment for a given Application System, especially in the areas of storage, network placement/connectivity, and security.

This discovery led to the creation of an additional strategy that had to be implemented to complete the vision to differentiate the CDS Cloud offering from its competitors. This strategy called for the development of another set of standard processes, which as far as is known, is the first and only standard Application Deployment Methodology (ADM). The ADM is a conceptual model used in project management that describes the stages involved in support of an ICT Infrastructure development and deployment project to gather the ICT Infrastructure requirements of the Application System(s) software to be deployed in a consistent, complete manner and to deploy the Application System(s) software in conjunction with a DMM project. ADM Documentation is crucial and is done in parallel with the DMM process.

The implementation of this strategy resulted in the ADM process being integrated into the Rainbow Chart of Processes, as shown in Figure 10.9, under the major process described in the ITIL framework as: Application Systems Management. The implementation of ADM resulted in an integrated process which provides consistent and complete ICT Infrastructure requirements needed to allow for the successful deployment and execution of a given Application System.

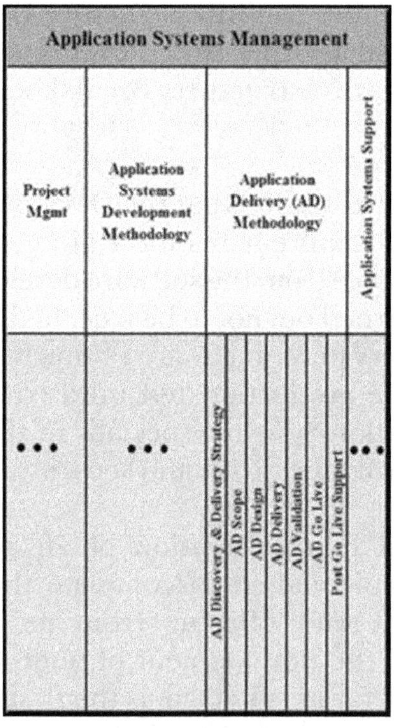

Figure 10.9: *The Application Deployment Methodology Sub-Process within I/S Rainbow Chart*

An Additional Change Driver

While analyzing External Influencing Factors, the I/S Division discovered a new IT Value Cycle which is based on MIT Survey results [21 and 22] that found that out of 18 common IT and non-IT management tasks, only four have a statistically significant correlation to business value provided by IT: Needs Identification, Business Process Re-engineering/Organizational Change, Application Development, and IT Oversight to ensure the successful integration of these three, as illustrated in Figure 10.10.

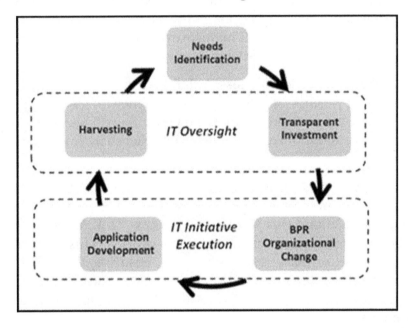

Figure 10.10: *Tasks with Significant Correlation to Business Value*

The I/S Division determined that this value-oriented focus model should be adapted to enhance their existing vision of creating IT Value through the delivery of *low-cost quality services* in claims processing, back-office processing, and hosting within the healthcare insurance business. Under this adaptation, an IT organization should look to provide IT Value to its clients in one of three areas:

- **Run-the-Business**: Value is delivered in the context of essential, enabling, non-differentiated IT Services. This value will be measured in terms of cost and service level metrics that allow the businesses I/S supports to achieve their desired balance of cost and quality. Note that these types of business expenses and/or investments do not produce new revenue for the client's business

- **Grow-the-Business**: Value is delivered through improvement in business operations for existing business markets and customer segments of the client businesses I/S supports. This value will be measured in terms of reduced expenses or the delivery of improved customer value.

- **Transform-the-Business**: Value is delivered by helping the client businesses I/S supports enter new markets with new value propositions aimed at new customers. This value will be measured in terms of increased market share and revenue.

The adaptation of this model involved changes to the LOB Management process within the Business Perspective Process Group. To facilitate this shift, a new process *IT Value Management* has been added to the LOB Management process. This new process will cover the primary responsibility for ensuring that *client business value* is a major consideration in selected I/S work efforts. The diagram in Figure 10.11 illustrates the shift in emphasis that this represents.

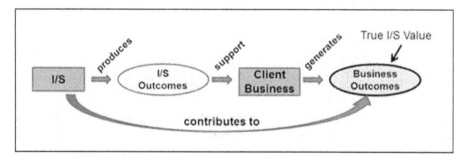

Figure 10.11: *The Shift to Additional Focus on Business Outcomes*

It is the responsibility of LOB Management to measure the following types of IT Value and to ensure that clients know the outcomes and view them as successful to their business. Figure 10.12 illustrates.

- **IT Value for Credibility** reporting:
  - Based on a more traditional value model of the delivery of low-price/cost quality services that provide the day-to-day support of the client's business (*Run-the-Business*)
  - Contains data which should be trended over time to help assess value

- **IT Value for Money** reporting:
  - Based on added business value provided by IT during the addition of new business-driven capabilities within Application Systems supporting the client's business (Grow-the-Business, Transform-the-Business)
  - Determined based on Business Executives, Business Management, and IT that are involved in the implementation of a specific IT Initiative participating in a structured post-implementation collection and review process (referred to as Harvesting) conducted over a specified period of time using a Harvest Team (which is not the same as the Project Team) to measure the value delivered from the initiative

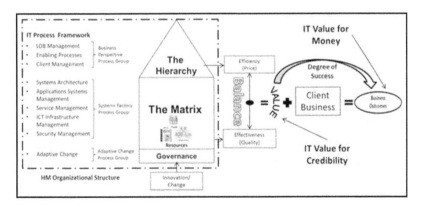

Figure 10.12: *Ensuring IT Value for Credibility and IT Value for Money*

The detailed strategies to accomplish the new value propositions are based on what must change to move from the "Old Reality" to the "New Reality" of IT value as adapted from [21] and illustrated below.

Old Reality: The IT organization should not have to talk about its performance, it speaks for itself.

New Reality: People see only what affects them most and this usually involves problems.

What Must Change:

Constantly measure and publish IT organization performance in terms that connect the performance to the businesses being served.

Old Reality: IT is a cost of doing business.

New Reality: If IT is only a cost, then it's something to constantly be reduced.

What Must Change:

Never convey cost without conveying value and performance.

Old Reality: IT delivers great technology for the enterprise.

New Reality: Technology is not an outcome for the businesses being served.

What Must Change:

IT Value comes from changing the outcomes and performance of the businesses being served.

Old Reality: Nothing as complex as IT can be perfect.

New Reality: Perfection in IT may not be possible, but excellence is.

What Must Change:

The IT organization should proactively share the businesses pain when things do not go well, do whatever it takes to minimize the pain, and show visible steps to prevent such incidents from happening in the future.

Old Reality: If the business does not follow the IT organization's rules and standards, IT will not guarantee that implemented changes will work.

New Reality: Business executives tend to focus on current, visible risks related to not pursuing current specific business opportunities. Hence, they are less likely to embrace the positive trade-off of shifting some resources to continually evolve the existing technology base into a smoothly functioning, well-design technology platform which provides the foundation for producing future less specific benefits.

What Must Change:

The IT organization must help business leaders see the rationale for IT rules and standards through the establishment and explanation of a technical architecture that helps guide the enterprise as its technical base evolves over time.

Old Reality: The customer is always right.

New Reality: The IT organization needs to play the role of 'peer' rather than 'subordinate'.

What Must Change:

The IT organization should help the business being supported to focus on what it needs to deliver to improve outcomes and performance, not just on what it asks for.

Old Reality: The success of business change is the responsibility of business executives.

New Reality: Business executives see business process and organizational change as a shared responsibility of IT.

What Must Change:

Business executives who know they need to make change happen, look to IT to help them understand exactly what change can be the most effective and why.

Old Reality: The IT organization must build complete solutions that work perfectly from the start.

New Reality: Business executives tend to believe that 'good enough' is a good place to start and then improve as the business grows.

What Must Change:

IT needs to stop designing and building the ultimate technical solution and focus instead on building a 'good enough' solution for the business to start and then improve as the business grows.

In summary, we have produced the Nine Major Process Groups for IT in Table 10.2 as it is configured *after the change initiatives were implemented.* Figure 10.13 depicts the Rainbow Chart of Processes with refinements as it was also configured *after the current change initiatives were implemented.* Note that associated with the Rainbow Chart of Processes is the new set of processes which are not part of the Nine Major Process Groups for IT, but represent the general processes for which a client of IT is responsible. In ITIL, this is referred to as 'The Business'. The final section of this chapter gives the definitions of the processes within the Rainbow Chart of Processes as they are shown in Figure 10.13.

Table 10.2: Updated Nine Fundamental IT Process Groups with Example
First-Level Refinements (after change initiatives)

IT Process Framework

Adaptive Change
Process Group

1. **Adaptive Change**
   - IT Governance
   - Audit Management
   - Quality Assurance

Business
Perspective
Process Group
(The Hierarchy)

2. **Line of Business Management**
   - Financial Management
   - Resource Acquisition
   - Client Business Sales Cycle Support
3. **Enabling Processes**
   - Managing People Program
   - Administrative tasks
4. **Client Management**
   - Relationship Management
   - Steering Support (Client Work requests)
   - Product Improvement
   - Systems/Service Monitoring
   - Internal Marketing

System Factory
Process Group
(The Matrix)

5. **System Architecture**
   - Application Systems Architecture
   - ICT Infrastructure Architecture
   - Research and Development
6. **Application Systems Management**
   - Project Management
   - Application System Development and Maintenance
   - Application Delivery Methodology
   - Application System Support
7. **Service Management**
   - Service Support
   - Service Delivery
8. **ICT Infrastructure Management**
   - Infrastructure Deployment Management
   - Operations Management
   - Technical support
9. **Security**
   - Plan Security
   - Implement Security
   - Evaluate Security
   - Maintain Security

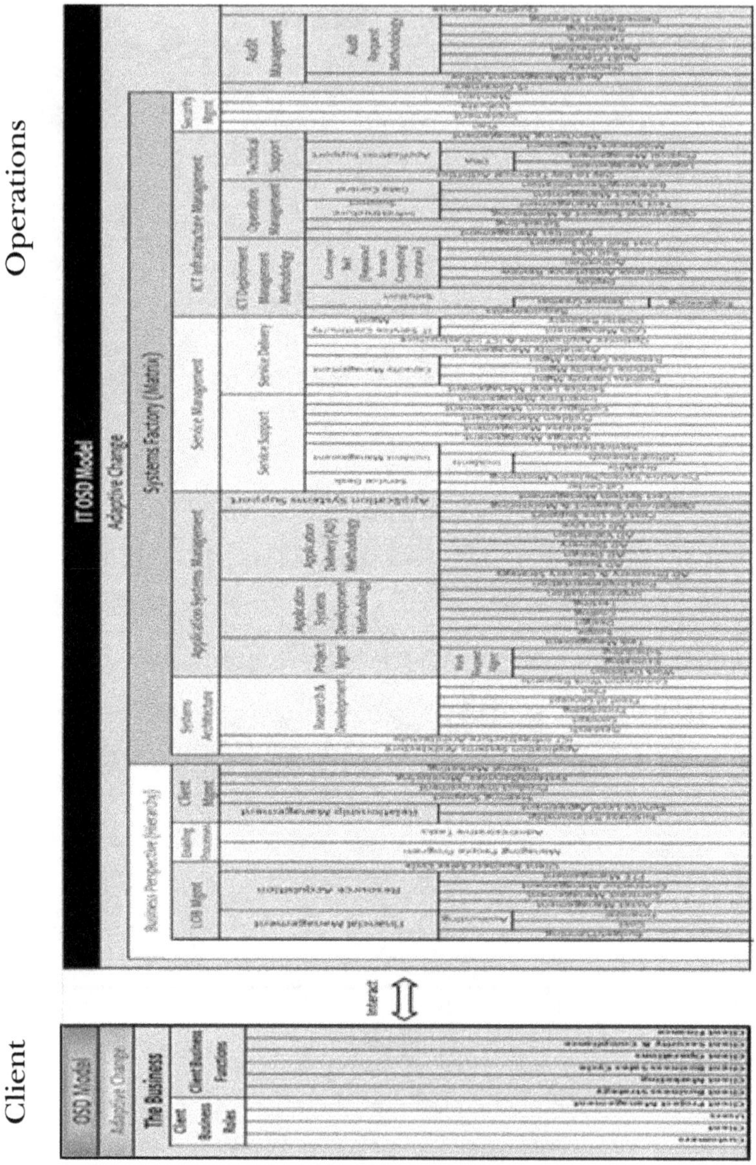

Figure 10.13: *The I/S Division Rainbow Chart (as of December 2015) with Lower-level Refinements and Client Business Interaction*

Leverage the Culture

Once the Rainbow Chart of Processes has been modified and the organization has devised appropriate associated strategies, a framework for change is complete. Now the strategies must be implemented successfully. Successful implementation requires not only a compelling vision and sound well-thought strategies, but also excellent execution. This execution occurs within the organization's culture.

The important thing to note about the I/S Division's approach to these transformative changes is that the needed strategies have been articulated within a familiar context. The organization has been utilizing the Rainbow Chart of Processes for many years to structure and guide the execution of its work. The Rainbow Chart of Processes has proven robust enough to accommodate the required process changes in a graceful manner, while still keeping intact the fundamental processes with which all staff are familiar. Further, the use of a specialization strategy that associates roles with higher level processes provides a natural bridge to assigning and accomplishing the new work within the modified Rainbow Chart of Processes.

Working within this modified process framework provides an excellent roadmap and important checks and balances for those working to implement the changes. Further, no new or modified Guiding Principles were required. Hence the basic tenets of the I/S culture remain unchanged. These factors taken together provide a very tangible psychological safety net to minimize the natural survival and learning anxieties that accompany any transformative change initiative.

Figure 10.14 captures the essence of the overall transformative change initiative, illustrating the central role that leadership plays as well as the importance of culture and the guiding frameworks provided by the IT-OSD Model and the Rainbow Chart of Processes.

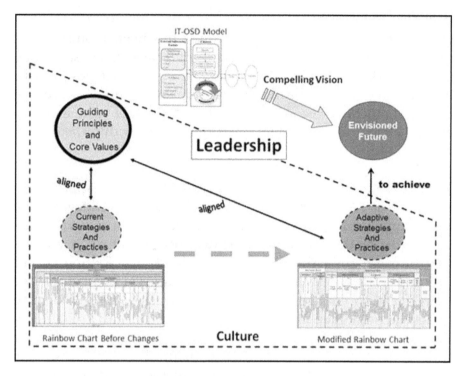

Figure 10.14: *The Overall Change Initiative Process*

The Rainbow Chart of Processes: Definitions

Recall that in dealing with the vision that an IT Organization should always operate in the 'business within a business' model, the I/S Division implemented a new strategy that encompassed implementing more precise definitions for the interactions between 'The Business' and 'The Business View' components of the ITIL Framework and the processes that support these interactions.

These new definitions and processes which described the needed Client Business processes for interaction with the Rainbow Chart of Processes do not comprise a component of the I/S Rainbow Chart of Processes proper, but instead reside *within the Client Business* to facilitate the client's ability to effectively interact with the Rainbow Chart of Processes.

The definitions of these general processes for which all client types are responsible were previously described and shown in Figure 10.7.

The reader will also recall that in responding to three major change drivers, the I/S Division made some significant changes to the Rainbow Chart of Processes itself. These changes were exhibited in Figure 10.13.

It should be noted that within the Nine Major IT Process Groups, the level and nature of process refinement as well as the degree to which the various refined processes are applied will depend on the specific needs and focus of any particular IT organization. In other words, within the Nine Major IT Process Groups, there is flexibility to allow each IT organization to choose to implement sub-processes according the needs of their individual environments.

The modifications made over the past several years by the I/S Division reflects the robustness of the Nine Major Process Groups to accommodate significant and transforming change within an IT organization. The descriptions below give **definitions of the processes** within the Rainbow Chart of Processes as these are currently configured in the I/S Division of BCBSSC.

IT-OSD Model: The IT Organizational System Design Model is based on the OSD Model introduced by Paul Gustavson and modified by BCBSSC to specifically help IT organizations better evaluate and understand the connections between various organizational design factors as they seek to achieve a design that will produce outcomes that support their strategic goals. This model provides an *overall framework* for assessing the need for adaptive change for the organization.

Adaptive Change Process Group: Processes for supporting adaptive change in the organization.

1.0   Adaptive Change

The Adaptive Change Component recognizes the need for a process to allow for innovation and adaptation within an organization's administrative and operational areas. Change is more easily adapted by establishing a governance process over both technical and administrative practices and processes.

1.1   I/S Governance

The I/S Governance process consists of persons comprising committees who make up a governing body for the purpose of authorizing technical and management standards and practices documented within I/S Governance manuals.

1.1.1   Quality Assurance

A process which examines, evaluates, and analyzes IT technical policies and management practices to ensure they are working effectively to improve the overall performance of the organization.

1.2   Audit Management

Processes related to conducting audits of I/S by internal and external entities to ensure that the information systems supporting a Client organization can respond flexibly to the audit needs in the Client's market.

1.2.1   Audit Management Office

Processes related to client management, serving as liaison between auditors and I/S, and to ensuring audit requests are completed on time, within budget, adhere to high quality standards, and ensuring that all audit findings or observations are either successfully rebutted or remediated.

1.2.2 Audit Request Methodology

Processes supporting a structured audit execution methodology (life cycle) defining the expectations and deliverables of I/S during the course of an audit.

1.2.2.1 Discovery

Processes related to gaining an understanding of the application or process that is to be audited so that the scope of the audit can be determined.

1.2.2.2 Audit Planning

Processes related to refining estimates, schedules and resource plans by I/S so that the appropriate level of support can be provided for the remainder of the audit.

1.2.2.3 Data Collection

Processes related to the gathering of any documentation or reports required to conduct the audit activities.

1.2.2.4 Fieldwork

Processes related to the auditing of the defined processes and/or artifacts against the established criteria, and the testing of control objectives.

1.2.2.5 Reporting

Processes related to the publishing of audit findings, the creation of responses and corrective action plans to the findings.

1.2.2.6 Remediation Planning

Processes related to ensuring that each corrective action has clear ownership and that the appropriate work effort is established for each item in the corrective action plan.

Business Perspective Process Group: Processes within Line of Business (LOB) Management and Client Management for supporting IT clients.

2.0 Line of Business (LOB) Management

LOB Management is the processes concerned with helping the I/S business assess whether its I/S service is doing the best it can with the money it has. All areas within the I/S organization are financially accountable to LOB Management for the costs charged to a given Client. LOB Management has financial accountability for all I/S costs charged to a given Client's LOB.

2.1 Financial Management

Processes to promote the wise and cost-effective use of IT resources in the pursuit of Client business goals.

2.1.1 Budget/Planning

Processes related to the annual Planning and Budgeting cycle.

2.1.2 Accounting

Processes related to the systematic recording, reporting, and analysis of financial transactions of an IT Organization as a business.

2.1.3 Cost

Processes within accounting where all cost incurred in carrying out an activity or accomplishing a purpose within an IT organization are collected, classified, and recorded and uses money as the economic factor of production. These processes must provide the ability to assign costs of an IT Service proportionally and fairly to the users of that service, this is referred to as "Charging or Allocating Costs". This data is then summarized and analyzed to provide financial transparency to gauge the efficiency of the IT service provision and to aid management in decision making processes to determine areas where cost savings could be made and or to aid in setting a selling price for said services.

2.1.4   Financial

Processes within accounting that monitor and control money as it flows in and out of an IT Organization in terms of assets, liabilities, revenues and expenses and that also gathers and summarizes financial data to prepare financial reports such as balance sheet and income statements to measure the economic performance of the IT organization.

2.2   Client Business Sales Cycle Support

Processes related to IT Application or Infrastructure System Architect (s) participating in a "Fit and Bid" assessments and also to interfacing with the Request for Solution (RFS) process which provides the IT Solution and its estimated costs for a new or expanded Client business opportunities.

2.3   Resource Acquisition

Processes related to the acquisition of all resources utilized by I/S.

2.3.1   Asset Management

Processes related to the approval of physical asset acquisition.

2.3.2   Contract Management

Processes related to the negotiation, approval, and monitoring of third-party contracts associated with I/S assets or services.

2.3.3   Contractor Management

Processes related to the approval of contractor employee acquisitions.

2.3.4   Full-Time Employee (FTE) Management

Processes related to the approval of FTE acquisitions.

3.0   Enabling Processes

Processes that define a complete system of acquisition, care, and treatment of IT human resources.

3.1   Managing People Program

A comprehensive program of general processes, programs, and information sources that are involved in effectively managing the IT people asset.

3.2   Administrative Tasks

Processes related to administrative tasks not already defined as an administrative process.

4.0   Client Management

Processes to establish and maintain relationships and ensure appropriate Client communication, Client focus and Client control of priorities by coordinating with the Client organization at strategic, tactical, and operational levels.

4.1   Relationship Management

Processes that foster relationships between the Client and the I/S organization.

4.1.1 Business Relationship

Processes that analyze problems, settle disputes, and negotiate with the Client within current contractual boundaries.

4.1.2 Service-Level Agreement (SLA)

Processes to ensure that the IT services required by the Client are continuously maintained and improved at an acceptable cost through designing, agreeing, and maintaining the following external documents: Service Level Requirements (detailed definitions of Client IT service needs), Service Level Agreements (non-technical agreement between Client and IT which details the service(s) to be provided), Service Level Catalogs (detailed non-technical descriptions of operational services and associated service levels offered by IT).

4.2 Steering Support

Processes that define how to work with the Client to understand their business needs as they relate to specific changes the Client wants in IT products and services, help the Client define these needs as specific changes, and work with the Client on priority setting.

4.3 Product Improvement

Processes that add value to the Client's business by discovering high-payoff opportunities to employ the proper subsets of an IT organization's products and services.

4.4 Systems/Services Monitoring

Processes that monitor the use and effectiveness of an IT organization's products and services for the Client on a day-to- day production basis by monitoring service levels, reporting actual versus agreed to service levels, and reviewing service levels with the Client to determine opportunities for improvement.

4.5 Internal marketing

Processes that define proactive communication programs concerning the IT products and services used by a given Client, and the potential use of additional products and services by a given Client.

System Factory Process Group: Processes for designing, implementing and supporting IT solutions for any of the IT Clients. The System Factory is divided into: Systems Architecture, Application Systems Management, Service Management, and Information Communication Technology (ICT) Infrastructure Management.

5.0 System Architecture

Process that defines what IT products or services are required to meet the Client's business needs, how they are to be provided, what IT Resources they require, and what common components can be leveraged across many Clients.

5.1 Application Systems Architecture

Process that identifies what IT products or services are to be provided, how they are to be provided, and what common components can be leveraged across all the IT organization's Clients. Includes evaluation of vendor Application Software features and costs.

5.2 Information and Communication Technology (ICT) Infrastructure Architecture

Processes for designing and maintaining strategies for the Information and Communication Technology Infrastructure that include all computing platforms, networks, operating systems, and enabling software.

Includes evaluation of all ICT Infrastructure features and costs.

5.3 Research and Development

Processes related to the investigation of new technology, Client business functionality, or IT processes for IT products or services.

5.3.1 Research

Process to study and establish facts about technology, business system architecture, and evaluate I/S strategic direction.

5.3.2 Concept

Process of defining a concept, I/S product or service based on the Research.

5.3.3 Prototyping

Process of creating a model and the simulation of the relevant aspects of an I/S product or service to evaluate the viability of a proposed solution.

5.3.4 Proof of Concept

Process of gathering and documenting sound evidence that the proposed solution related to an I/S product or service is feasible and viable.

5.3.5 Pilot

Process of conducting an initial limited roll out of a final solution into a production or operational environment, to validate the solution is working as designed.

5.3.6 Commission Work Requests

Process of commissioning the work requests to fully implement the I/S product or service.

6.0 Application Systems Management

Processes that define the creation, changing, or installation of Application Systems to insure that the information systems supporting a Client organization can respond flexibly to changes in the Client's market.

6.1 Project Management

Processes related to planning, monitoring and controlling, and integrated management of the Application Systems Development Methodology (ASDM) to ensure work requests are delivered on time, within budget, adhere to high quality standards, and meet Customer expectations.

6.1.1 Work Request Management

Processes related to Estimating, Work Scheduling, and IT Resource Management for work requests that take the form of change or project requests.

6.1.1.1 Work Definition

The process to define the high level business needs from a client's request for I/S work.

6.1.1.2 Estimating

Processes related to the estimation of effort to complete a given work request.

6.1.1.3 Scheduling

Processes related to planning and scheduling a given work request for completion.

6.1.2 Task Management

Task Management serves as the foundation for project management activities. Task Management is the process of managing, through its life cycle, an activity or collection of activities that need to be accomplished within a defined period of time or by a deadline, in order to meet pre-defined goal.

6.2 Application Systems Development Methodology (ASDM)

Processes supporting a structured systems development methodology (life cycle) to administer all aspects of requirements definition, design, and building or procurement of an application.

6.2.1 Scope

Processes related to the creation of a document that contains the business needs and functional requirements for a given work request. Requirements development is accomplished within the scope process of the Application Systems Development Methodology and the corresponding processes of the ICT Deployment Methodology.

6.2.2 Design

Processes related to the creation of a document that contains the specifications of how to satisfy the functional requirements for a given work request, conform to the limitations of the target medium, meet implicit or explicit requirements on performance and resource usage, and satisfy any restrictions on the design process itself, such as its length or cost. Requirements management, the technical solution, and verification processes are accomplished throughout the design process of the Application Systems Development Methodology and the corresponding processes of the ICT Deployment Methodology.

6.2.3   Coding

Processes related to the creation or modification of application software or the procurement of application software. Requirements management, the technical solution, and verification processes are accomplished throughout the Coding process of the Application Systems Development Methodology and the corresponding processes of the ICT Deployment Methodology.

6.2.4   Testing

Processes related to the evaluation of application software to ensure that it complies with the requirements of a given work request. The requirements management process is accomplished throughout the testing process. The technical solution and verification processes are accomplished throughout the unit testing process, and the product integration and validation processes are accomplished throughout the system testing process of the Application Systems Development Methodology and the corresponding processes of the ICT Deployment Methodology.

6.2.5   Implementation

Processes related to the creation of a document that contains the requirements and tasks to deploy into Production application software associated with a given work request. Product integration and validation processes are accomplished throughout the implementation process of the Application Systems Development Methodology and the corresponding processes of the ICT Deployment Methodology.

6.2.6 Post--Implementation

Processes related to corrective actions allowed for a given work request during a fixed time period after implementation. Product integration and validation processes are accomplished throughout the post-implementation and closure processes of the Application Systems Development Methodology and the corresponding processes of the ICT Deployment Methodology.

6.3 Application Delivery Methodology (ADM)

Processes related to the delivery and validation of external applications and any corresponding support operation or services that are required for a particular business.

6.3.1 AD Discovery and Delivery Strategy

Processes associated with defining the Delivery Strategy in terms of Application Delivery Management work requests to meet the requirements related to providing the required production and test infrastructure execution environments and the other related Factory operational support and monitoring processes for an application. This is accomplished through the validation related Request For Solution (if one exists) to the signed contract or change order, obtaining and analyzing the Application Surveys, conducting application and business interviews, and determining responsible ownership for delivery elements.

6.3.2 AD Scope

Processes related to defining the business, functional, technical, and operational requirements for a given ADM Work Request. The output of this phase is an AD Scope Document.

6.3.3 AD Design

Processes related to defining the approaches and specifications for how to satisfy the business, functional, technical, and operational requirements and to satisfy any restrictions on the design process itself (such as length or cost) for a given ADM Work Request. The output of this phase is an AD Design Document.

6.3.4 AD Delivery

Processes related to the installation, configuration and/or modification of the required Factory operational support and monitoring processes as documented in the AD Design Document for an ADM Work Request.

6.3.5 AD Validation

Processes related to the validation of the delivered platforms, technologies, and tools and other Factory related operational support and monitoring processes for a given ADM Work Request to ensure they comply with the defined requirements.

6.3.6 AD Go Live

Processes related to the implementation of the required production and test infrastructure execution environments, the Application and other related system factory operational support and monitoring processes from an end-user perspective.

6.3.7 Post Go Live Support

Processes related to corrective actions allowed for a given Application Delivery Management

Work Request during a fixed time period after Go Live.

6.4 Application System Support

Processes related to the operations and support of our Production and Test application systems.

6.4.1 Operational Support and Monitoring

Processes related to the operational support and monitoring of Production application systems, as well as service requests which are I/S generated.

6.4.2 Test System Management

Processes related to the support and management of Test application systems, as well as service requests which are user generated.

7.0 Service Management

Processes related to providing the operational products and services required to meet a Client's business needs.

7.1 Service Support

Processes that allow Clients (the person(s) authorized to conclude an agreement with the IT Organization about the provisions of IT Service, and ensuring IT Services are paid for, the "pay the bill" people) and Users (people in the Client Organization that use the IT Services for their routine activities, the "hands on the keyboard" people) to get access to the appropriate IT services to support their business.

7.1.1 Service Desk

The single point of contact for Production application or deployed infrastructure environment incidents and service requests. The Service Desk's main purpose is to resume "normal service" to the User as soon as possible. This may be resolving a technical error, dispatching an incident for resolution, filling a service request or answering a User question.

7.1.1.1 Call Center

Processes related to responding to calls or contacts concerning incidents, providing information to Users, and authorizing or resetting passwords.

7.1.1.2 Pro-Active System/Network Monitoring

Processes related to pro-actively monitoring application system execution and the ICT Infrastructure.

7.1.2 Incident Management

A reactive process with the goal of returning to a normal level of service, as defined in a Service Level Agreement. This is accomplished by the business activity of a Client Organization and its Users with the smallest possible impact.

7.1.2.1 Incident

Processes related to the recording, monitoring, and closure of any event which is not part of the standard operation of a service, and which causes or may cause an interruption to or a reduction in the quality of that service.

7.1.2.1.1 Critical Research

Processes that respond to day-to-day Production System incidents that involve requests for detailed technical research from the Applications

Systems or Infrastructure areas, and result in the identification of manual workarounds, or the execution of a Break/Fix process.

7.1.2.1.2 Break/Fix

Processes related to the alteration or normal repair of a failure in the infrastructure or application systems. These processes include an escalation process based on operational system downtime or impact of failure.

7.1.2.2 Service Request

Processes related to the fulfillment of requests from a User for support, delivery, information, advice, or documentation as defined as a "standard service" under an SLA which is not related to a failure in the infrastructure or would result in the alteration of the application or infrastructure.

7.1.3 Change Management

Processes related to managing all Requests for Change (RFCs) that are not defined as a standard service under a Service Level Agreement, and are associated with a work request, error correction request, or Infrastructure Architecture modification request.

7.1.4 Release Management

Processes related to the planning, preparation, and scheduling of a "release set," which is a collection of authorized changes, defined by Work Requests and Requests for Changes (RFCs).

7.1.5 Problem Management

Problem Management is the processes concerned with the detection of the underlying causes of an incident by focusing on the identification of problems based on Incident Analysis and transforming those problems into "known errors." Once problems are identified, the focus changes to their subsequent resolution and prevention.

7.1.6 Configuration Management

Processes that provide direct line of sight into IT Assets related to Application Systems, ICT Infrastructure, and Life Cycle Documentation configuration items used in the provision of live, operational services.

7.1.7 Inventory Management

Procedures related to all IT asset (hardware and software) Procure, Receive, Deploy, Maintain, Retire, and Harvest.

7.2 Service Delivery

Processes that ensure the Client obtains the services (a combination of availability and use of Production systems in which IT and Client interact or participate simultaneously - the experience cannot be assessed in advance, but only when the service is provided) needed to support their business.

7.2.1 Service Level Management

Process of monitoring and reporting actual versus SLA levels for review by Client Management with Clients on a regular basis and to ensure that the

IT services required by the Client are continuously maintained and improved at an acceptable cost. This is accomplished through designing, agreeing, and maintaining the following internal documents: Service Specification Sheets (describes the relationship between functionality agreed to by a Client and the technology implemented by IT), Operational Level Agreement (agreements with internal IT departments detailing the provisions of certain elements of service), and Underpinning Contracts (contracts with external suppliers detailing the provision of certain elements of service).

7.2.2 Capacity Management

Processes to ensure the required capacity for data processing and storage is provided at the right time and in a cost-effective manner to support the agreements made with IT Clients.

7.2.2.1 Business Capacity Management

A proactive process to understand the current and future needs of a Client's business by analyzing strategic plans, marketing plans, etc. to gather business forecast data in terms of units of work to be processed as defined by the business.

7.2.2.2 Service Capacity Management

A proactive process to understand the use of IT products and services by the Client and to gather data to compare to SLAs.

7.2.2.3 Resource Capacity Management

A proactive process to determine the use of the ICT Infrastructure and components in terms of resource capacity.

7.2.3   Availability Management

Processes related to providing a professional response and solution to undesirable situations (i.e., when availability levels are measured and a difference between supply and demand is negative). Monitors Mean Time to Repair, Mean Time Between Failures, Mean Time Between System Incidents, and Percentage Availability by Client.

7.2.4   Optimize Applications and ICT Infrastructure

Processes to review and evaluate the performance of Application Systems and ICT Infrastructure based on data obtained from Capacity Management, Availability Management, and System Monitoring and Analysis. The focus is on compliance with the defined analytics and opportunities for improvement in service to Clients, or to reduce costs.

7.2.5   IT Service Continuity Management

Supports the overall Business Continuity Management of a given Client by ensuring that required IT Infrastructure and IT Services (including Application Systems) can be restored within specified time limits after a disaster.

7.2.5.1   Crisis Management

Procedures related to the centralized management of recovery operations for any event that is not part of the standard operation of a service, and which has caused an interruption to or a reduction in the quality of that service.

7.2.5.2   Disaster Recovery

Procedures related to the restoration of original performance levels of a service or system within specified time limits after an event, where significant effort is required to restore the original performance level. This is to ensure that accurate and functional recovery plans and procedures are in place for all Application and ICT Infrastructure assets.

8.0 ICT Infrastructure Management

Processes needed to provide a stable data processing and communication infrastructure that is aligned with Client(s) business needs at acceptable costs.

8.1 ICT Deployment Management Methodology (DMM)

Processes which are built on the strategy of leveraging a standard set of highly integrated and automated processes related to Information Communication Technology (ICT) Infrastructure deployment to create a unique differentiation from competitors within the 'managed cloud services' market space. The processes define a structured development methodology (life cycle) and supported by a highly scalable automation system to administer all aspects of requirements definition, design, and building, testing, implementation and turnover for any ICT Infrastructure platforms.

8.1.1 Requirements

Process related to the discovery and documentation of technical business requirements and involves the following inputs:

- An Application Survey for each Application must be completed or updated and becomes part of permanent Systems Documentation.

- An Application Survey must be completed or updated for each standalone Tool (Application or ICT) or ICT Technology and becomes part of permanent Tool or Technology Documentation.

- Concept Diagram must have all Applications, standalone Tool or Technology that will be modified or created to satisfy the Requirements listed by SMI ID and cross-referenced to the Concept Diagram.

8.1.2 Solutions

Processes related to the design, documentation and implementation of the relationship between:

1) An Application System

2) A standalone Tool (Application or ICT)

3) ICT Technology upgrade, and an existing, required Service Offering which is comprised of the **Computing Instances** and when applicable the **Leveraged Platform Instances** needed to deploy the specific infrastructure **Solution** used to completely execute an instance of an Application, Tool(s), or ICT Technical Upgrade

8.1.2.1 Service Creations

Processes related to creation or modification of a Service Offering and related Network Profiles.

8.1.2.1.1 Engineering

Processes related to the engineering of a Service Offering and related Network Profiles:

- A **Service Offering** is a pre-architected and pre-engineered grouping of standardized infrastructure elements as defined within **SMI** that comprise the wide variety of

computing platforms sup-
porting business applica-
tions or standalone Tools
that can be reused in the
deployment of **Computing
Instances** (CIs) and/or
**Leveraged Computing
Instances** (LPIs) to support a given Application
or standalone Tool.

- **Network Profiles** define
the types of approved
communication for a giv-
en network entity in terms
of network ports, proto-
cols and services. Profiles
are analogous to logical
zones – able to support
discrete tenants and maintain security compliance.

8.1.3 Pre-Orchestration Processes

Process related to reserving ICT infrastructure
assets to be used in the deployment of specified Computing Instances and/or Leveraged
Computing Instances for a given Application or
standalone tool within a given ICT Solution and
issuing the associated 'build' instructions to be
used in the Conveyer Belt Process.

8.1.4 Orchestration Processes (also called Conveyer Belt). Note: Repeated for each Computing Instance

Processes related to the deployment of the ICT
infrastructure components comprising the computing instances required to support a given
Infrastructure Solution associated with a given

application or standalone Tool instance or ICT Technology update.

8.1.4.1 Deploy

Processes supporting the Virtual and/ or Physical deployment of the ICT infrastructure components related to the Service Offerings that are required to support a given computing instance (IE: Unit Test, System Test, QUAL Test and Production) associated with a given application or standalone Tool instance or ICT Technology update.

8.1.4.2 Compliance Acceptance Review

Processes related to the evaluation of the newly deployed infrastructure to ensure it meets security and audit requirements of the Infrastructure Solution.

8.1.4.3 Activation

Processes related to the transfer of knowledge to ensure our operational organizations are prepared to support the newly deployed Infrastructure Solution.

8.1.4.4 Roll Out

Processes related to the operational roll out of the newly deployed Infrastructure Solution.

8.1.4.5 Post Roll Out Support

Processes related to the correction actions taken during a fixed period of time after operational Roll Out to support of the newly deployed Infrastructure Solution.

8.2 Operations Management

For any and all computing platforms, the day-to-day management and maintenance of the ICT Infrastructure which includes Facilities Management, Scheduling, Operations Support and Monitoring, Test System Management, Output Management, and Balancing & Reconciliation.

8.2.1 Facilities Management

Processes related to the day-to-day management of the facilities housing ICT Infrastructure.

8.2.2 Scheduling

Processes that manage the entire Application Systems workload for any given business process within the ICT Infrastructure.

8.2.3 Infrastructure Support

Processes related to the operations and support of our Production and Test Infrastructure systems.

8.2.3.1 Operational Support and Monitoring

Processes related to the operational support and monitoring of Production Infrastructure systems, as well as service requests which are I/S generated.

8.2.3.2 Test System Management

Processes related to support and management of Test Infrastructure systems, as well as service requests which are user generated.

8.2.4 Data Controls

Processes related to the management of Production System output.

8.2.4.1 Output Management

Processes related to both online access to and physical delivery of Production System output.

8.2.4.2 Balancing/Reconciliation

Processes that define Production System balancing procedures and the overseeing and monitoring of system out-of-balance issues until the conditions are resolved and all clean-up activities are completed.

8.3 Technical Support

For each computing platform, there are processes and functions that develop expertise about the current and future operational properties, systems, management tools and configuration of the ICT Infrastructure.

8.3.1 Day to Day Technical Activities

Processes related to maintaining technical skills, supporting Incident, Problem, Configuration, Availability Management, and Research & Evaluation.

8.3.2 Application Support

Processes defined to provide technical assistance to Application System specialists in the use of the ICT Infrastructure.

8.3.2.1 Database Administration (DBA)

Processes related to the design and maintenance of database structures.

8.3.2.1.1 Logical Management

Processes related to the design and maintenance of the

manner in which data is presented to application programmers or Users of the data.

8.3.2.1.2 Physical Management

Processes related to the design and maintenance of the manner in which data is physically recorded on hardware.

8.3.3 Middleware Management

Processes related to the management of software that mediates the interaction between disparate applications across heterogeneous computing platforms.

8.3.4 Monitoring Management

Processes related to the creation, changing, installation and support of Enterprise Monitoring Systems to collect data in an active and/or passive mode concerning the network, the end user's experience and computing platforms.

9.0 Security Management

Processes related to providing the needed level of security taking into consideration internal requirements as well as meeting the security requirements specified in SLAs and external contractual or legal requirements.

9.1 Plan

Processes related to the definition and design of IT organization's security activities within the framework of highly developed repeatable administrative and operational processes.

9.2 Implement

Processes related to the creation or modification of the IT organization's security activities within the framework of highly developed repeatable administrative and operational processes based upon the approved plan.

9.3 Evaluate

Processes related to the monitoring and evaluating the efficiency and effectiveness of security-related activities, policies, procedures and controls.

9.4 Maintain

Processes driven by the results of the security compliance evaluations to propose improvement action plans for security-related activities, policies, procedures and controls.

References

(In order of citation)

1. Steve Wiggins and Ken Abernethy, *Picasso on a Schedule: The Art and Science of Managing IT, Part 1* (North Charleston, SC: Create Space, 2012).

2. Steve Wiggins and Ken Abernethy, *Managing Picasso: The Art and Science of Managing IT, Part 2* (North Charleston, SC: Create Space, 2014).

3. Kotter: "What Leaders Really Do," *Harvard Business Review,* December 2001 (originally published in 1990).

4. John Zenger and Joseph Folkman, *The Extraordinary Leader,* (New York: McGraw-Hill, 2009).

5. Frederick Herzberg, Bernard Mausner, and Barbara Snyderman. *The Motivation to Work* (New York: John Wiley and Sons, 1959).

6. Edgar Schein, *Organizational Culture and Leadership,* 4th *Edition,* New York: McGraw-Hill, 2010).

7. Sonja Sackman, *Assessment, Evaluation, and Improvement: Success through Corporate Culture,* (Heidelberg: Verlag Bertelsmann Stiftung, 2006).

8. Frederick P. Brooks, Jr., *The Mythical Man-Month: Essays on Software Engineering, Silver Anniversary Edition* (Boston: Addison-Wesley, 1995).

9. Susan Cain, *Quiet: The Power of Introverts in a World That Can't Stop Talking* (New York: Broadway Paperbacks/Random House, 2012).

10. Gregory Berns, Chappelow J.C., Zink C.F., Pagnoni G., Martin-Skurski M.E., and Richards R., "Neurobiological Correlates of Social Conformity and Independence during Mental Rotation" *Biol. Psychiatry* 58, 2005.

11. Adrian Furnham, *The Psychology of Behavior at Work* (Hove, East Sussex, UK: Psychology Press, 2005

12. Mihaly Csikszentmihalyi, *Creativity: Flow and the Psychology of Discovery and Invention,* (New York: Harper Collins, 1996).

13. GregoryFeist, "Autonomy and independence," *Encyclopedia of Creativity, Vol. 1* (San Diego, CA: Academic Press, 1999).

14. Tom DeMarco and Timiothy Lister, *Peopleware: Productive Projects and Teams, 2nd Edition,* (New York: Dorset House Publishing, 1999).

15. Michio Kaku, *The Future of the Mind,* (New York: Anchor Books, 2015).

16. Sir Winston Churchill's "We Shall Fight on the Beaches" Speech, retrieved on September 24, 2015 from https://en.wikipedia.org/wiki/We_shall_fight_on_the_beaches.

17. Sir Winston Churchill's "Finest Hour" Speech, retrieved on September 24, 2015 from https://en.wikipedia.org/wiki/This_was_their_finest_hour.

18. Jim Collins, *Good to Great* (New York: Harper Business, 2001).

19. Mike Pedler, John Burgoyne, and Tom Boydell, *The Learning Company: A Strategy for Sustainable Development* (New York: McGraw-Hill, 1996).

20. Peter Senge, *The Fifth Discipline: The Art and Practice of the Learning Organization* (New York: Doubleday Business, 1994).

21. Richard Hunter and George Westerman, *The Real Business of IT,* (Boston: Harvard Business Press,2009).

22. George Westerman and Peter Weill, "Getting Business Value from IT: The Non-IT Executive View," *MIT Sloan CISR Research Briefings, V1(3A),* 2006.

Appendix

Behaviors Characterizing the Differentiating Competencies for IT

This Appendix provides listings of the behaviors characteristic of all the 19 differentiating competencies. Note that three (#'s 6, 10 and 16) of the competencies apply only for Hierarchy Leaders. For the remaining competencies that apply to both the Hierarchy and the Matrix Leaders, some characteristic behaviors apply only to Hierarchy Leaders. These are italicized, and all other behaviors apply to both Hierarchy and Matrix Leaders.

Competency 1:

Hierarchy Leader: Displays High Integrity and Honesty

Matrix Leader: Displays High Integrity and Honesty

Characterizing Behaviors:

- Avoids saying one thing and doing another
- Follows through on promises and commitments
- Models the core values
- Leads by example

- Can be trusted by others to "do the right thing" as it relates to other people

- Honest and ethical when dealing with others, especially when using company resources

- Demonstrates ethical resolve in adverse circumstances

- Accepts responsibility for success and failure

Competency 2:

Hierarchy Leader: Strategic Technical Leadership

Matrix Leader: Technical/ Professional Expertise

Characterizing Behaviors:

- Stays up to date in the field

- Demonstrates technical, functional and job-specific knowledge required for assignments

- Sought out for opinions, advice and counsel

- Knows the job well

- Understands the technology and profession well

- Makes significant contribution toward achieving team goals through knowledge and skills

- Uses technical knowledge to help team members troubleshoot problems

- Develops credibility with teammates because of in-depth knowledge of issues or problems

Competency 3:

Hierarchy Leader: Issues Resolution

Matrix Leader: Solves Problems and Analyzes Issues

Characterizing Behaviors:

- Collects data from multiple sources when solving a problem
- Asks the right questions to obtain the information needed to size up a situation properly
- Obtains accurate and crucial information as a basis for sound organization-wide decisions
- Systematically evaluates information by using a variety of proven methods and techniques
- Encourages alternative approaches and new ideas
- Encourages others to seek and try different approaches for solving complex problems
- Sees patterns and trends in complex data and us the patterns to outline a path forward
- *Coaches others on how to analyze information to solve problems and make decisions*
- *Clarifies complex data or situations so that others can comprehend, respond and contribute*
- *Proactively shares data with others to help them analyze situations*

Competency 4:

Hierarchy Leader: Innovates

Matrix Leader: Innovates

Characterizing Behaviors:

- Consistently generates creative, resourceful solutions to problems

- Constructively challenges the usual approach to doing things and find new and better ways to do the job

- *Acts as a champion for ingenuity at all levels*

- *Generates creative solutions by bringing together the most talented people*

- *Works to improve new ideas rather than discourage them*

- Comes up with creative, resourceful solutions to problems

- *Creates a culture of innovation and learning that drives individual development*

- *Provides support and encouragement to others when they attempt to innovate—even when they fail*

- Integrates ideas and inputs from different sources to find innovative solutions

- Builds on others' suggestions and ideas

Competency 5:

Hierarchy Leader: Practices Self-Development

Matrix Leader: Practices Self-Development

Characterizing Behaviors:

- Seeks feedback from others to improve and develop

- Makes constructive efforts to change and improve based on feedback from others

- Constantly looks for development opportunities

- Continually develops depth and breadth in key competencies

- Demonstrates a curiosity toward learning

- Takes ownership for self-development

- Looks for ways to build challenge into current assignments
- Learns from both success and failure
- Models self-development and embrace its value
- Committed to continuous personal self-development

Competency 6:

Hierarchy Leader: Decision-Making

Matrix Leader: N/A

Characterizing Behaviors:

- *Confidently and decisively makes own decisions*
- *Correctly assesses the risk and return of decisions*
- *Demonstrates sound judgment in decision-making*
- *Uses negotiation skills to resolve problems early*
- *Anticipates and addresses potential problems early*
- *Facilitates employee self-reliance in problem solving*
- *Involves team members in problem-solving and decision-making when appropriate*

Competency 7:

Hierarchy Leader: Drives for Results

Matrix Leader: Drives for Results

Characterizing Behaviors:

- Aggressively pursues all assignments and projects until completion
- Does everything possible to meet goals and deadlines

- Consistently meets or exceeds commitments

- Follows through on assignments to ensure successful completion—doesn't lose interest before a project is completed

- Holds others accountable for achieving results

- *Leads or champions efforts to increase productivity and goals accomplishment throughout the organization*

- *Holds people accountable*

Competency 8:

Hierarchy Leader: Establishes Stretch Goals

Matrix Leader: Establishes Stretch Goals

Characterizing Behaviors:

- Generates agreement among group members on achieving aggressive goals

- *Builds commitment with all employees on team goals and objectives*

- Fosters the confidence of others that goals will be achieved

- Promotes a spirit of continuous improvement

- Maintains high standards of performance

- *Sets measurable standards of excellence for yourself and others in the work group*

Competency 9:

Hierarchy Leader: Takes Initiative

Matrix Leader: Takes Initiative

Characterizing Behaviors:

- Volunteers for challenging assignments

- *Uses discretionary time to help others uncover opportunities or solve problems*

- Goes above and beyond what needs to be done without being told

- Has the confidence to initiate action independently

- Independently addresses unexpected problems or opportunities

- *Anticipates and responds to external threats or opportunities before they affect business performance*

- Models proactive behaviors

- Takes personal responsibility for outcomes

- Can be counted on to follow through on commitments

Competency 10:

Hierarchy Leader: Resource Planning and Management

Matrix Leader: N/A

Characterizing Behaviors:

- *Helps people understand how their work contributes to broader business objectives*

- *Puts the right people in the right places at the right time*

- *Properly manages budgets and timelines*

- *Correctly allocates resources across competing priorities*

Competency 11:

Hierarchy Leader: Organizational Leadership/ Communication

Matrix Leader: Communicates Powerfully and Prolifically

Characterizing Behaviors:

- Communicates clearly and concisely
- *Delivers effective presentations and speeches*
- *Uses strong writing and verbal skills to communicate facts, figures and ideas to others*
- Skillfully communicates new insights
- *Breaks down communication barriers between teams and departments*

Competency 12:

Hierarchy Leader: Coaching/ Inspiring Others

Matrix Leader: Inspires Others to High Performance

Characterizing Behaviors:

- Has a personal style that helps to positively motivate others
- Energizes people to go the extra mile
- Skillfully persuades others toward commitment to ideas or action
- *Effectively exercises power to influence key decisions for the benefit of the organization*
- *Employs different motivational strategies to influence the behavior of others*
- Inspires others to support organizational priorities

Competency 13:

Hierarchy Leader: Business Relationships

Matrix Leader: Builds Relationships

Characterizing Behaviors:

- Seen as approachable and friendly
- Establishes rapport easily
- Trusted by work group members
- Handles difficult situations constructively and tactfully
- Deals effectively with people in order to get work accomplished
- *Balances concern for productivity and results with sensitivity for employees' needs or problems*
- *Maintains and utilizes relationships outside the company through which resources or information can be generated*
- *Properly manages relationships with third parties*
- Sensitive to the needs of others

Competency 14:

Hierarchy Leader: People Process Management/ Staff Development

Matrix Leader: Develops Others

Characterizing Behaviors:

- Acts as a coach or mentor to facilitate learning from experience
- *Fosters a learning environment that encourages others to learn from their experience*

- *Finds stretch assignments for individuals which require them to achieve significant but realistic goals*

- Gives honest and candid feedback in a helpful way

- *Makes the tough people decisions necessary to ensure current and future success*

- Creates a development plan and works hard on acquiring new skills

- Open to feedback from others

- *Willingly gives challenging development goals*

- Willingly shares his/her time to help others develop

- Proactively shares new ideas and job knowledge with others

- *Displays a strong commitment to staff development*

- *Correctly evaluates potential in others*

- *Delegates tasks based on qualifications and ability*

- *Selects employees with the skills and experience necessary to meet job requirements*

- *Recognizes employee training needs and provides/coordinates training*

Competency 15:

Hierarchy Leader: Flexibility/ Collaboration/ Teamwork

Matrix Leader: Collaboration/ Teamwork

Characterizing Behaviors:

- Promotes a spirit of cooperation with other members of the work group

- Champions an environment that supports effective teamwork

- Has the trust and respect of the team

- Develops cooperative working relationships with others in the company

- Takes into account how individual actions affect the team

- Fosters a climate of trust and respect within the team

- *Removes barriers to positive team performance*

- Proactively addresses conflicts and disagreements that affect team effectiveness

- Models teamwork by working effectively with other leaders in the organization

- *Ensures that the work unit works well with other groups and departments*

- Comfortable with ambiguity

- Adapts to changing circumstances

Competency 16:

Hierarchy Leader: Delegation

Matrix Leader: N/A

Characterizing Behaviors:

- *Builds commitment in others for their individual and team objectives*

- *Gives clear, understandable instructions to employees and others*

- *Creates clear work plans and timetables*

- *Allocates resources to maximize effectiveness*

Competency 17:

Hierarchy Leader: Strategic Thinking

Matrix Leader: Broad Perspective

Characterizing Behaviors:

- Knows how work relates to the organization's business strategy

- Balances the short-term and long-term needs of the organization

- Demonstrates forward thinking about tomorrow's issues

- *Proposes initiatives that become part of the organization's strategic plan*

- *Clarifies vision, mission, values and long-term goals for others*

- *Translates the organization's vision and objectives into challenging and meaningful goals for others*

- Ensures that work group goals are aligned with the organization's strategic goals and vision

- *Explains to others how changes in one part of the organization affect other organizational systems*

- *Sets and articulates a compelling vision for the organization*

- *Continually communicates the highest-priority strategic initiatives to keep the leadership team focused on the right things*

- *Ensures that all systems in the organization are aligned toward achieving the overall strategic goals*

- *Leads organizational efforts that exploit highly leveraged business opportunities*

Competency 18:

Hierarchy Leader: Manages Change

Matrix Leader: Supports Change

Characterizing Behaviors:

- Acts as a change agent—strongly supports the continual need to change

- *Champions projects or programs, presenting them so that others support them*

- *Is an effective marketer for work group projects, programs or products*

- Energizes others to want to change by pointing out the need for change

- *Encourages people to let go of old ways so new ways can begin*

- *Lets others know how change will positively affect them*

- Helps teams and work groups translate new change goals into practical implementation steps

- *Champions organizational change initiatives in a way that helps people understand, appreciate and support them*

- Helps others overcome their resistance to change

- *Creates a compelling case for change*

- *Fosters an organizational climate that creates business structures and systems for supporting change initiatives*

- *Makes sure people understand the links between change initiatives and the organization's strategic business direction*

Competency 19:

Hierarchy Leader: Connects the Group to the Outside World

Matrix Leader: Connects the Group to the Outside World

Characterizing Behaviors:

- Knows how to deliver products or services that delight customers by meeting and exceeding their expectations

- *Uses knowledge and feedback from an external perspective to improve products and services*

- Views work in the context (through the eyes) of the external customer

- Helps people understand how meeting customer needs is critical needs is central to the mission and goals of the organization

- *Translates first-hand knowledge of customers into organizational strategy, goals and direction*

- *Demonstrates the ability to represent the work group to key groups outside the group or department*